Les Femmes de bonne Humeur. Liturgie. Les Contes Russes. La Boutique Fantasque. Parade. Pulcinella. Le Chant du Rossignol. Cuadro Flamenco. Cloud. La Belle au Bois dormant. Renard. Noces. Les Tentations de la Bergère. Les Biches. Les Fâcheux. Cimarosiana. Le Train Bleu. Zephyr et Flore. Barabau. Romeo and Juliet. La Pastorale. Jack in the Box. Le Triomphe de Neptune. La Chatte. Mercure. Le Pas d'Acier. Ode. Apollon Musagète. Le Bal. Le Fils Prodigue

DIAGHILEV
AND THE BALLETS RUSSES

BORIS KOCHNO

DIAGHILEV
AND THE
BALLETS RUSSES

TRANSLATED
FROM THE FRENCH BY
ADRIENNE FOULKE

DESIGNED BY
BEA FEITLER

HARPER & ROW, PUBLISHERS
NEW YORK & EVANSTON

Excerpts from Diaghilev's letters to
Stravinsky quoted on pages 101, 186 and 189 appeared
in slightly different form in *Memoirs and Commentaries.*
Copyright © 1960 by Robert Craft and Igor Stravinsky.
Reprinted by permission of Alfred A. Knopf, Inc.

The illustrations reproduce material
in the collection of Boris Kochno, which was photographed
for this book by Niki Ekstrom.

FIRST EDITION. LIBRARY OF CONGRESS CATALOG CARD NUMBER: 70–123945

Frontispiece: Ballets Russes program, 1923, by Picasso

To Parmenia Migel Ekstrom
without whose loving care
this book would never have
been conceived, written and
hence finally published.

Boris Kochno

Flyleaf of the first copy of the Ballets Russes program, 1923,
inscribed by Diaghilev to Boris Kochno, thanking him for his
devoted labors in producing "a work which will, at last, testify
truly to my long endeavors."

CONTENTS

DIAGHILEV
AND THE BALLETS RUSSES

THE
ORIGINS OF
THE
BALLETS RUSSES

ALEXANDRE
BENOIS

Unpublished text
of an article written at the request
of Boris Kochno

The Ballets Russes can be considered a part of the famous export campaign undertaken, entirely at his own risk, by Serge Pavlovich de Diaghilev, one of the most remarkable and outstanding figures of the early twentieth century. Well before 1909, the year of his first ballet season, Diaghilev had demonstrated his abilities as an organizer of exceptional energy and talent. It was he who had contrived to knit us young Russian painters into a homogeneous group, he who organized our first exhibitions, he who founded the influential art magazine *Mir Isskoustva* (*The World of Art*) in St. Petersburg, which wrought an altogether radical change in the aesthetic standards of Russian society; it was he again who organized the splendid exhibit of Russian portraiture that entirely filled the immense Tavrida Palace. But all this activity took place in Russia, and was aimed at raising the artistic understanding of Diaghilev's compatriots. It was not until 1906 that he inaugurated what I have called his "export campaign."

How can one define the reasons that spurred Diaghilev toward this undertaking? I think I am not wrong in tracing his motives to a profound patriotism that animated him as well as his close friends. This feeling was not expressed in theories or platforms or slogans, however. Perhaps we ourselves were not fully aware of our motives, and assuredly we felt only an ironic hostility for all official patriotism. We found countless things to object to in the conditions of life in Russia, and were quick to criticize them mercilessly. Nonetheless, we could not help but love our country or fail to respond to the strange charm of her soul, and all our activity was aimed at glorifying Russian art— indeed, everything around us in Russia that held beauty and spiritual meaning.

THÉATRE
de
L'HERMITAK.

But Diaghilev had personal reasons also for transferring his activity abroad and devoting himself entirely to the exportation of Russian art. The time came when he no longer found in his own country enough scope and freedom for his nature, temperament, and ambitions to function. Like all young men of his class, Diaghilev had started his career by entering government service (in 1899). His beginnings were brilliant indeed. He was appointed Official for Special Missions under the new director of the Imperial Theatres, Prince Serge Volkonsky, who was also a personal friend.

Diaghilev carried out handsomely the first special assignment he received, which was to edit the *Annual Report of the Imperial Theatres* for the year 1898–99. Heretofore, this had been an utterly bureaucratic publication, lacking any artistic quality. Diaghilev took advantage of the intellectual resources around him to produce a book of exceptional elegance and taste which was full of altogether priceless artistic and historical documents. The publication was a great success; all the truly cultivated members of St. Petersburg society took an interest in it, and even the Czar expressed his great satisfaction to Prince Volkonsky. A most brilliant future was opening before Diaghilev, but unfortunately his very success proved fatal. He immediately committed one of those faux pas that are seldom excused in a subordinate. Confident in his success, in February, 1901, Diaghilev presented his director with conditions that the latter could not accede to, his friendship and admiration for Diaghilev notwithstanding. The misunderstanding between them took on a bitter tone, and within a week Diaghilev found himself "dismissed," which was tantamount to being excluded from any state employment in the future. * All his hopes—and ours with them—seemed to collapse beyond recall.

More serious still, Diaghilev did not enjoy the Czar's favor. Nicholas II distrusted strong-willed and gifted personalities. The imperial attitude did not change even after the historic portrait show, although the exhibition showed Diaghilev to be a man of exceptional cultivation, capable of directing large-scale enterprises and giving every evidence of an ardent desire to serve his country. At thirty, Diaghilev saw himself condemned to almost total inactivity; he was suffocating, and quite naturally he began to look about for a wider field of action.

Struck by the fact that not even the names of our early or our modern painters were known outside Russia, he resolved to transport some of their works to Paris, then the center of fashionable life. And thus it was that, for five brief weeks, Paris could see a collection of the most characteristic examples of Russian art, from sixteenth- and seventeenth-century icons to paintings by contemporary artists. The collection was shown in the galleries of the Grand Palais, which were specially decorated for the occasion after sketches by our friend Léon Bakst. For my part, Diaghilev entrusted me with putting together the illustrated catalogue and, despite my aversion for any and all public appearances, insisted that I deliver an address at the opening.

---

* Thanks to his connections, Diaghilev managed to become an exception to the rule, and a year after this catastrophe he was attached to His Majesty's Chancellory. This post, while highly prestigious, was both obscure and boring, and could not console him for his banishment from the theatre, for which he felt he had a true vocation.

Diaghilev's second "export campaign" consisted of the concerts of Russian music he presented at the Paris Opéra, in which our most celebrated artists and virtuosi took part. Unfortunately, these very fine concerts met with rather indifferent success. Even we, who were the instigators and organizers, were not satisfied with them; our whole group loved music passionately, but we conceived of it more as the integrating element of a stage spectacle, whether opera or ballet. All our activity up to that point had been devoted to the plastic arts—through the publication of our two art magazines (I had launched the second, *Treasures of Russian Art*, in 1901), exhibitions, books, and stage design. Concerts by their very nature are, as spectacles, rather dull. Therefore we decided, in that spring of 1907, that for the next Paris season we would bring Russian opera to Paris, and, after some hesitation, our choice fell on Moussorgsky's *Boris Godunov*. Its production at the Paris Opéra in the spring of 1908 was most sumptuous. The sets were made after sketches by Golovine, Juon, and me; the magnificent costumes were created after designs by the great specialist in early Russian art, Stelletsky, and Diaghilev personally scoured the antique shops for everything he could find, from peasant caps to old brocades. The enterprise appealed to me above all for its audacity. We did not encounter the same good will everywhere, and often we had to cope with all sorts of treacherous intrigues, but, in the end, the obstacles were swept away thanks to the genius, tact, and diplomacy of Diaghilev. When all Paris gathered for the première, it was amazed by the beauty of the performance. This success encouraged Diaghilev and his group to undertake other productions, which in every respect surpassed the first.

In the autumn of 1907, a few months after the Paris concerts and a few months before the presentation of *Boris*, an old dream of mine had come true in St. Petersburg, one result of which was the transportation of Russian ballet to Paris, following the opera. The old dream was the creation of a ballet whose subject and mise-en-scène would express my own ideas and be devised by me alone. It was a dream that I had nurtured since adolescence, indeed since childhood. In 1887, at the age of seventeen, I had begun to compose a ballet on a subject I had found in a collection of German tales; in many ways, it was analogous to Fouqué's *Undine*—the same theme that much later would inspire Jean Giraudoux to write one of his most charming plays. This "Chain of the Nixie" ("*Die Kette der Nixe*") I translated into a ballet in three acts of five scenes. I began ardently to compose the score and simultaneously to design the sets. My ballet was full of fantastic romanticism and dramatic vicissitudes; like my two favorite ballets, *La Bayadère* and *Giselle*, it concluded with the deaths of all the characters.

At moments, my friends and I felt we were witnessing the birth of a remarkable masterpiece, but once I had finished my score, I was disheartened. My work seemed childish; its similarity to everything I had until then enjoyed in the theatre seemed to me laughable. So I put my "Nixie" aside, and presently everything I had invented faded from my memory. But it was a first attempt, a first hint of what was to be for me and my friends the creation of our "Ballets Russes."

Yet I never did stop dreaming of a ballet spectacle that I would create all by myself. The music was the thing that always brought me up short. Every day I used to improvise for hours on end, but I no longer attached the slightest importance to this daydreaming, for I realized that I was quite ignorant of musical theory. So, everything that flowed from my fingers—and sometimes it was not without grace or charm—was swiftly doomed to oblivion. Among my close friends, I did not find one professional musician who could come to my rescue. Walter Nouvel, A. P. Nourok, and Diaghilev were devoting themselves more systematically to music (the first two were later to found the Society of Contemporary Music). Yet Nouvel, after composing some strange songs in ultramodern style, withdrew permanently into silence. Nourok sometimes regaled us with musical fragments that had a kind of precious charm, but he never succeeded in advancing beyond these isolated attempts. As for Diaghilev, he definitely abandoned musical composition as early as 1895.

———————

And then suddenly I found a collaborator in the person of a very cultivated and gifted young man who had studied with Rimsky-Korsakov and was a recent brilliant graduate of the Conservatory. This was Nicholas Tcherepnine. Personally, he stayed apart from our group, but I came to know him after his marriage to my elder brother's daughter. When he learned that I wanted to create a ballet, Tcherepnine offered to work with me, and he soon discovered that we had certain tastes in common: he shared my enthusiasm for E. T. A. Hoffmann, whom I had admired from earliest youth. I even had a penchant for making the appreciation of my favorite author serve as an infallible criterion of character, and I blithely divided people I met into those I thought understood Hoffmann and those I thought did not. Unfortunately, I found no subject for my ballet in this poet's work, but I found one in another of my favorite Romantics—Théophile Gautier. One of his stories, imbued with the Hoffmannesque spirit, became the point of departure for my plot. I told Tcherepnine of my find; he shared my excitement and, a few weeks later, brought me several themes that delighted me with their color, verve, and poetry. My ballet was issuing from limbo, and its future outlines were already becoming clear.

However, it was not to see the footlights so quickly. The new director of the Imperial Theatres, Vladimir A. Telyakovsky, appeared to take a lively interest in our project, but this happy beginning was followed by a contretemps that lasted for several years. Disregarding simple prudence, I had several times expressed in the press, in very biting terms, my opinion of new Imperial Theatre productions, and they happened to be the very ones that Telyakovsky had personally directed, and whose success he especially banked on. Our relations suffered, inevitably, and I became this gentleman's bête noire. Then came the years spent with my family abroad, in Rome, Versailles, and Paris, and I completely stopped thinking of my *Pavillon d'Armide*. Tcherepnine, on the other hand, remained in St. Petersburg and, in moments of leisure, continued to work on his score. The young ballet master Michel Fokine, then on the threshold of his career, was looking for some heretofore unperformed ballet that he could stage for the graduation exercises of the students at the Imperial School. Tcherepnine had meanwhile become orchestral director for ballet performances, and he suggested a finished segment of his score. Fokine and Tcherepnine had occasion to meet almost daily onstage or in the rehearsal studios, and the two young artists grew to be friends.

The graduation exercises, held in the spring of 1907, elicited an enthusiastic public response, which led Alexander Krupensky to take an interest in our ballet. This young state official, acting on the authority vested in him by Telyakovsky (who was on temporary leave), decided to produce *Le Pavillon d'Armide* in its complete form for the forthcoming season at the Imperial Maryinsky Theatre. Tcherepnine, who had come to Paris on business of his own, told me this good news and, what is more, said that Krupensky intended to make me responsible for the sets, costumes, and general supervision of the work. When I returned to St. Petersburg after being away for three years, I was received with open arms by Krupensky and immediately everything got under way for the staging of our ballet. With the help of two good assistants, I undertook to paint the sets I had designed, the opera wardrobe staff began to execute the sumptuous costumes, and the prop workshop started on the production of the headgear, crowns, and decorations needed for the costumes and props. All this was in order to invest the central scene of the ballet, which took place in the fantastic gardens of the magician-king Hidraot, with a splendor that would recall the fêtes of the Sun King, whom I greatly admired and to whom I had dedicated several paintings.

Presently I met Fokine. From our first conversation, his lively enthusiasm charmed me; he asked nothing better than to hear every kind of suggestion from me, in the light of which he almost entirely altered his original mise-en-scène. This second version was generally thought to surpass the first, both in magnificence and in dramatic development. The company (with a few exceptions) was delighted and predicted our complete success. As for the three coauthors, for months we were in a state of creative fever, exchanging ideas and, in the course of our work, introducing entire scenes that we had never envisaged earlier. As originator of the ballet's theme and author of the book, I retained unchallenged the major direction of our work. The production developed in an atmosphere of mutual understanding and friendliness, and it is this that contributed particularly to its exceptional freshness and brilliance.

Although we got along perfectly well among ourselves, not everything proceeded smoothly with regard to the theatre management. People who had come to know Krupensky better had warned me from the outset about his capricious moods, his temperamental nature, and his arrogance, but I felt secure in the welcome he had extended to me and did not attach much importance to these comments. Suddenly, without our learning why, Krupensky's attitude changed. Possibly Telyakovsky's antipathy for me had something to do with it, but more than anything else it was the unforeseen expenses the mise-en-scène entailed, which he had not fully assessed at the start and which must have caused him the keenest anxiety. From then on, a veritable battle was waged between Krupensky and me. To save my work, I appealed to people who were in a position to put pressure on the management. I even went so far as to arrange for a long and bitter interview in the most widely read newspaper in St. Petersburg to bring the matter to public attention. These steps proved effective.

At one point, however, our production seemed to be in such difficulties, and the management so averse to having *Le Pavillon d'Armide* succeed, that the celebrated star Kchessinska, who had rehearsed the major role and knew it to perfection, suddenly, for no plausible reason, withdrew a few days before the première. Our friendship with Pavlova saved the day. That magnificent artist volunteered to replace her colleague, and certainly we did not suffer thereby. Pavlova was then in the full flower of her youth and beauty; her queenly bearing and the innate nobility of her movements and of her dance style were assets we had no reason to regret. The other performers were also at their best. My efforts to have Paul Gerdt perform in my ballet had been motivated by a kind of sentimentality; I very much wanted as the young male lead in "my first ballet" the artist whom I had so enjoyed applauding when I was still a child. On this occasion, I mustered enough tenacity to overcome my favorite's objections on the grounds that he was too old (Gerdt was then skirting his sixties). When it came to the proof, it was clear that I had been right to persist. The role was a complete success for Gerdt, and once again he confirmed the reputation for eternal youth he had made for himself by creating premier-danseur roles in our ballet for almost half a century.

It is impossible not to mention, in the same breath with Gerdt, the name Nijinsky. This very young artist, fresh from the Imperial School, had not yet had the opportunity to reveal his gifts to the public. But Fokine knew perfectly well what Nijinsky was capable of, and insisted that he have a part in *Le Pavillon d'Armide*. It was on his account that I introduced a character not previously planned for—the Favorite Slave of Armide. The role provided Nijinsky with the chance to take part in the ensemble dances and scenes. Furthermore, Fokine created a special solo for Nijinsky, to Tcherepnine's music; it opened with a standing leap, very high and sustained, the feet held together—a feat no one else in the company could have achieved. Nijinsky managed this leap with an amazing ease, grace, and simplicity—seemingly without the slightest effort. For me, Nijinsky's plasticity was a revelation. He was a young, rather stocky man—not at all beautifully proportioned—and was, furthermore, so timid that he seemed rather to fade into the background. At rehearsals, he made anything but a good impression. But footlights, a costume, transformed him. Where did such suppleness, grace, and ease of gesture come from? Onstage, he created an impression of enchanting beauty, which was as evident in the role of Armide's slave as it was in his analogous role in *Schéhérazade* a year later.

Following my accusatory newspaper interview, the management decided to demonstrate publicly how unfounded my attack had been, and gave us a week for two additional full rehearsals. It was to one of these that I invited S. P. Diaghilev, who was agog to see our work. Thereupon an incident occurred I had not even remotely foreseen: the commandant of the theatre guards approached my friend and ordered him to leave the theatre instantly. Telyakovsky wanted to deal harshly with the man he considered a particularly dangerous and detestable rival. My protestations and threats were all in vain: Diaghilev was forced to leave the auditorium, and did so, but he was deeply wounded. That was probably the moment when he felt most violently the desire to triumph over his enemies and to show the world what he was capable of. And the future would show things in their true light. The world-wide fame of Russian theatrical art is inseparable from the name of Diaghilev, while it owes nothing to the Telyakovskys and Krupenskys. . . .

But Krupensky had not yet conceded defeat, and he tried to take his revenge at the very last moment. He placed the première of *Le Pavillon d'Armide*, which consisted of three scenes lasting an hour and a half, at the end of the evening's program, following Tchaikovsky's *Swan Lake*—a very long and complex ballet that was always, everywhere, except in Russia, cut to half its length. It would have been a simple matter to give our ballet with another short one—*Ruse d'Amour* or *Les Saisons*—but such was the management's ill will toward us that, by ordering this particular double bill, it hoped part of the audience would leave after *Swan Lake* while the rest would be too tired to pay much attention to the new work that was being offered them. And, in point of fact, our ballet began at eleven and did not end until after midnight. No one, however, thought of leaving. From the opening bars, a fervor of curiosity pervaded the theatre, which always presages either a triumph or a fiasco. In our case, it was the former, an explosion of the audience's enthusiasm. My theme interested and touched them; my sets and costumes evoked thunderous applause; Tcherepnine's music, which he had orchestrated superbly, appealed powerfully through its poetic, mysterious quality; Fokine's dances and groupings were utterly beautiful. Despite the late hour, every number called forth prolonged ovations, and the "Encores!" of the audience forced us to repeat them. Pavlova, Gerdt, Nijinsky, and Rozai (who executed incredible feats in the dance of the clowns), and the charming and very young dancers Kyasht, Tchernicheva, and Karsavina all triumphed. It was one o'clock when the applause finally subsided, but still the audience could not bring itself to leave the theatre, and people massed at the door in a dense crowd, exchanging opinions and reactions. In a fever of excitement, Diaghilev shoved his way through the crowd to reach me and smother me in his arms. "This is what must be shown in Europe, this is what we will take to Paris!" he cried.

From that moment, not a day passed that Diaghilev did not revert to his idea: Russian art, and especially our ballet, which had no equal anywhere, had to be made known to the West. At the time (November–December, 1907), we were already much too busy with preparations for *Boris Godunov*, and it was impossible for us to undertake anything more. But the idea was there, maturing and acquiring substance. The success of *Boris* cleared away a thousand and one difficulties. Diaghilev could henceforth count on the support of the Czar's uncle, the Grand Duke Vladimir, to help us establish various useful connections and also to obtain for us the funds necessary to carry out our grandiose plans. The Grand Duke also considered it essential from the government's point of view for Russian art to triumph.

The selection of what would be sent to the Parisians in the spring of 1909 was not determined immediately. Only one thing was definite, and that was *Le Pavillon d'Armide*. The rest we discussed endlessly. We could count on Chaliapin for sure; he had created an unforgettable impression in the role of Boris, but the great artist's repertoire was not too varied. At last, we settled on Borodin's *Prince Igor*, in which Chaliapin would sing two roles—Prince Galitzky and the Khan Kontchak. Two of the sets were ordered from Nicholas Roerich and were painted immediately. But then we remembered the tremendous impression Chaliapin had made on us in Rimsky-Korsakov's *Pskovitianka*; also, it was for this opera that Golovine had designed his most beautiful décor. So the choice of *Pskovitianka* prevailed. However, Diaghilev decided to change its title, which would have meant nothing to a French public, and he substituted for it the name of the central character, *Jean le Terrible*. Again because of Chaliapin, we took Serov's *Judith*, for Holofernes was one of the singer's best roles.

But it was the choice of ballets that presented the biggest problems. A kind of veto prevented our choosing a work by our favorite composer, Tchaikovsky: Diaghilev did not want to defy the current tastes of the French public and critics. Glazounov's little ballets did not seem substantial enough, while the old "classical"—and interminable—ballets in the repertoire of the Imperial Theatres of St. Petersburg and Moscow were not at all satisfactory musically, and, after all, for us the quality of the music was a primary consideration. Diaghilev was so demanding that, in choosing Arensky's *Nuit d'Égypte*, to give more body to the oversweet and light music, he went so far as to introduce fragments lifted from *Russlan* by Glinka, *Mlada* by Rimsky, *Khovanshchina* by Moussorgsky, and *Les Saisons* by Glazounov; the final scene, completely revised, was accompanied by stage music in a tragic vein, specially commissioned from Tcherepnine for the occasion.

It was at my insistence that *Nuit d'Égypte* was chosen. At the moment, I was very close to

Fokine, who undertook no work without consulting me; we had even thought up and put together a very short ballet with characters from Italian comedy and music by Clementi, which was performed only once, at a ball organized by the students at the Academy of Fine Arts. I took an active part in making certain changes in the plot of *Nuit d'Égypte*, and certain ideas for the mise-en-scène in the St. Petersburg version were entirely mine. For example, I persuaded Fokine to leave Cleopatra and her lover onstage in the love duet when the cruel and voluptuous queen gives herself to the young man she has just met. I suggested that the couple be concealed by veils held in the outstretched hands of priestesses performing a ritual dance. The idea was very risqué, but we were living in a period which countenanced audacities that would have been impossible ten years earlier (and perhaps today too).

In Fokine's new mise-en-scène, *Nuit d'Égypte* was performed in St. Petersburg only once, and not as part of the repertoire of the Imperial Theatres. The production was subsidized by a benevolent society that had approached Fokine to give them something of his own choosing. At the time, Fokine was passionately interested in the ancient world, and he spent whole days in the Hermitage studying vases and sarcophagi. (The subject of his first ballet, *Eunice* [1904], had been taken from *Quo Vadis?* by Sienkiewicz.) Now he remembered a ballet that had been given previously without great success, and that had as its locale the land of the Pharaohs. Financial considerations prevented a complete revamping of the earlier mise-en-scène of this ballet; however, usable items were found in scenery and costume storage rooms and the patrons did agree to extra expenditures for certain numbers and for the leading performers. The Egyptian and Hebrew costumes, after designs by Bakst, gave the production a certain iridescence and enough historical plausibility. *

Fokine, the youthful reformer of Russian ballet, created his second masterpiece as a private commission and not for the management of the Imperial Theatres. He did not enjoy the management's good will; for that matter, they had suspected him of being a revolutionary ever since, on behalf of the permanent company, he made certain demands that had some political coloration. (This occurred during the troubled years 1905–6.) *Le Pavillon d'Armide* only exacerbated the friction between Fokine and his superiors, and their displeasure was further aggravated by the friendly ties that had developed between Fokine and "that dreadful Benois." Fokine saw himself relegated to inactivity, which is why, in the spring of 1908, he undertook to produce, for the same benevolent society, a suite of dances to music by Chopin. A year later, in Paris, this work was given the now traditional name of *Les Sylphides*. In January or February of 1909, Fokine staged *Nuit d'Égypte*, which we then rebaptized *Cléopâtre*, and in Paris this ballet won a success that was surpassed only by that of the *Polovetsian Dances* from *Prince Igor*.

---

* In Paris, Bakst was in complete charge of the mise-en-scène for *Cléopâtre*, as the ballet was then called. His sets, costumes, and props were exceptionally beautiful. Unhappily, none of these were to survive; apparently they were all lost during one of the company's tours. And because he was then at odds with Bakst, Diaghilev approached another painter for a new *Cléopâtre* mise-en-scène.

Our entire group particularly loved the music of *Prince Igor*, and it was with deep regret that, for various reasons, we found ourselves forced to exclude the complete opera from our Paris repertoire. However, Diaghilev did not have the courage to give up the *Polovetsian Dances*, and in retaining them, once again he revealed his special flair. It was precisely this half-ballet, half-opera production that raised audience excitement to its highest pitch. Parisians were delighted by the music, by the Asian brilliance of the ensemble, and by Roerich's poetic scenery, which represented a hot evening on the steppes. But what most aroused their enthusiasm was the kind of orgiastic madness Fokine was able to inculcate in the dancers. At the end, when Sophia Fedorova led the dance like one possessed, her companions, too, utterly in the grip of the music's frenetic rhythm, the orchestra conductor, Cooper, seemed about to leap over the footlights himself, while the audience jumped and shouted for joy. . . .

———————

Another big trump card in our Paris success was the appearance of Ida Rubinstein in our productions. Her engagement had been something of a gamble. None of us, not even Diaghilev, could be really sure about this young artist. Only Bakst had been present at the private lessons she was taking from Fokine. He enthusiastically assured us that this young society woman would give us full satisfaction in the mimed role of Cleopatra and that most certainly she would achieve a far more interesting effect than Ludmila Barach, who played the doomed queen in St. Petersburg. And indeed, when, to the strains of mysterious music, the young and divinely beautiful Ida appeared onstage, without her veils, in a regally sumptuous déshabillé designed by Bakst, we ourselves were enchanted from the very first rehearsal. As for the audience, it followed the long and very complicated ceremony of "unveiling" with mounting admiration. The entire scene of Cleopatra's arrival was my invention, but to Fokine belongs the credit for having carried out my intent with perfect tact and taste. The resurrection of the mystical beauty of ancient Egypt was expressed in an absolutely convincing way. As a result, Ida Rubinstein in *Cléopâtre* became the talk of Paris, and that most precious *arbiter elegantiarum* of the period, Robert de Montesquiou, publicly declared himself the young artist's admirer.

Even the admirable Pavlova was eclipsed by the triumph of Rubinstein. Pavlova arrived at the end of our season, and found no role that was truly to her advantage. She kept her old part in *Cléopâtre*, but she did indeed seem relegated to second place by the majesty and beauty of her rival.

In that spring of 1909, our success in Paris surpassed our most ambitious dreams. Yet the task had been far from easy. Our leader and his companions in arms had had great difficulties. At one point, our enterprise seemed shipwrecked. The Grand Duke Vladimir Alexandrovich, our principal Maecenas, who had done so much for the success of *Boris Godunov*, died suddenly, only a few months before we were to open our season. His widow, the Grand Duchess Maria Pavlovna, inherited from her husband the presidency of the Academy of Fine Arts, and at first expressed her firm intention of supporting us. But then, another of those characteristic faux pas of Diaghilev's offended her, and, from one day to the next, she refused him all moral and material assistance. It was a hard blow, and anyone but Diaghilev would have been floored, the more so because everything was already under way: the Théâtre du Châtelet had been leased and the artists' contracts signed; the sets were being painted after designs by Korovine, Golovine, Roerich, Serov, Bakst, and me; substantial sums of borrowed money had already been spent.

Our dancers were assembled for the first rehearsal, in the Hermitage Theatre adjoining the Winter Palace, where all of Fokine's preparatory work was to take place, when a flunky from the Court arrived to inform me that, on an order from a highly placed person, access to the hall was forbidden us and that we must leave. The maneuver seemed to me all the more cruel for being unexpected. The company was thrown into wild confusion. Fokine was in a rage; the future that had seemed so radiant had darkened and was beginning to look hopeless. Only our leader, who had been informed by telephone, did not lose his head. With unshakable faith in his own star, he promptly went in search of other work space, and within less than an hour, when the artists were already getting ready to go home, Mavrine—Serge's secretary—arrived to announce that a new place had been found and everyone was invited to go there forthwith. The foresighted Mavrine had even rented a whole fleet of carriages into which our ladies and gentlemen stepped, in groups of three or four; bringing up the rear came the wardrobe women with their huge baskets.

Serge had discovered a theatre that had just recently been refitted by some club and had not yet been used. The stage of the Salle Catherine proved to be deep and amply adequate for the movements of our dancers. The auditorium was lighted by a row of high windows; the lounge was a series of salons painted in the bright, gay colors fashionable at the time. Everything was spanking-new. As the company arrived, everyone was vastly pleased to find ready and waiting a buffet collation that Serge had had sent in from a nearby restaurant. Diaghilev and I, both slightly superstitious, thought we detected a promising omen in a handsome portrait of Catherine II that embellished the grand staircase. The benign smile of the Empress welcomed us graciously and seemed to be apologizing for the poor reception we had just been tendered in her Hermitage. Friends of our enterprise came to join us: the charming doyen of St. Petersburg balletomanes, the corpulent "General Bezobrazov"; the well-disposed ballet critic, Svetlov; Prince V. N. Argutinsky; and the Court physician, S. S. Botkin. Enthusiasm and gaiety reigned, and from then on became the habitual state of mind of the company and its leaders. No one any longer doubted our mission, and everyone fell to work with a zest seldom in evidence when it was a question of "serving the government."

This mood was even intensified when our "horde" arrived in Paris. The company was made up almost entirely of young people who, until then, had seen nothing but the streets of St. Petersburg and the walls of the Maryinsky and the Imperial Ballet School. Compared to these young people, we were old, although Diaghilev was then only thirty-seven and I thirty-nine. Everyone had to be lodged in hotels near the Châtelet, particularly in the Latin Quarter, about which the group had a vague idea from the novels of Dumas and Paul de Kock. I remember still the excitement of one young dancer when, from his mansard window, he first glimpsed beyond the roofs and chimneys the gray towers of Notre Dame. Also, it was not the sullen Paris of winter; it was Paris in the spring, the days were mild, and the trees were bursting into new leaf. The open-air stalls and the handcarts were heaped with flowers, the rays of the sun gilded the building façades, the pavements were filled with people, while cabs and private carriages and buses flowed in all directions. Paris offered herself in all her bewildering brilliancy, her overflowing life.

Even I, an "old Parisian of 1896," was made drunk by all this beauty. Unable to part company with my young friends, I arranged to take my meals with them between rehearsals. Not yet blasé about this small world, I came to know its special charm, which was composed of great artistic sensitivity and naïveté. On this "mad jaunt to Europe," these young people were coming into contact with a life that was infinitely freer and more colorful than the one they were used to. At the same time, they were passionately serious about their work, and they felt a kind of salutary terror as they awaited the scrutiny they would undergo in this "arena of the world." For the same reason, they worked with a spirit of discipline and enthusiasm that they had never shown in Moscow or St. Petersburg. Their director, Fokine, was likewise aware of his total responsibility; he did not spare them, training them with considerable severity, and demanding from his aide, Serge Grigoriev, the same intransigency—which, it may be said parenthetically, helped to make the latter the first-rate regisseur that he became.

———————

My own duties were as varied as they were undefined. It was not until 1911 that I agreed to assume (and for a short while only) the title of "artistic director" in the Diaghilev enterprise. But in actuality that is what I had been since the *Boris Godunov* production. Obviously, I gave special attention to my ballet, *Le Pavillon d'Armide*, but in that instance my task was somewhat simplified because the sets and costumes (which differed substantially from the Maryinsky mise-en-scène) arrived all complete from St. Petersburg, and I had only to adapt them to the Châtelet stage. Apart from that, however, it was in Paris that we worked out the definitive form of *Les Sylphides*, the suite of dances to orchestrated music by Chopin. For the set, I had imagined a deserted cemetery, near the ruins of a convent; this anticipated *Giselle*, which we gave, with my sets and costumes, the following year, in 1910. I also oversaw the execution, assembling, and lighting of the sets, which had been designed by my absent friends—Golovine, Korovine, Roerich, and Bakst.*

I saw to it that the costumes were fitted and worn exactly as the painters' sketches prescribed; in addition, I had to busy myself with certain indispensable visits and with interviews with the

———————

* Neither Golovine, Korovine, Roerich, nor even Bakst was present in Paris during the most feverish preparations for the season. I was especially heartbroken over Bakst's absence. God knows why, but Diaghilev, despite my repeated insistence, delayed bringing him on from St. Petersburg. However, Oreste Allegri, who had painted the new sets for *Le Pavillon d'Armide* after my sketches, was of priceless help to us and he became, as of then, a faithful collaborator in our enterprise.

press when and wherever our leader, who was submerged in work, could no longer manage all alone. I would go back to my rue Cambon hotel half dead from fatigue, and I had no respite until our opera and ballet premières were crowned with total success.

In saying that our company consisted only of young people, I completely forgot the presence among us of an authentic oldster: he was K. F. Waltz, chief stage manager of the Imperial Theatres, whom Diaghilev, rather mistrustful of the Châtelet personnel, had thought it wise to engage. Waltz had long since passed his sixties, but no one would have guessed his real age. A Don Juan of legendary fame, he unabashedly rouged his cheeks, dyed his mustaches, and sported a jet-black wig. At the same time, he was energy incarnate, and his ingenuity was boundless. He did not know the meaning of the word "fatigue"; at the theatre he would be the first to arrive and the last to leave—not to go back to his hotel to rest but to spend a part of the night in world-famous restaurants in the company of our most charming young women dancers. Always joking, Waltz was able to infect others with his good humor, from Chaliapin, who each night before his entrance would be gripped by unconquerable stage fright, to the least young girl in the corps de ballet. Waltz had brought several Moscow carpenters to Paris with him, and with their help he had put the Châtelet's plant into shape, for—strange as it may seem—it was rather primitive. *Le Pavillon d'Armide* called for two highly complicated, quick changes that necessitated setting up a whole system of traps in the stage floor. The magician Waltz having seen to this, everything went off in perfect order from the evening of the dress rehearsal on.

But it was with the fountains that Waltz surpassed himself! In St. Petersburg, the gardens of Armide had been provided with a single, rather puny jet of water. This did not seem adequate to Waltz, who, to astound Paris, constructed two fountains—one on each side of the stage. Heavy columns of water, illuminated by spotlights, rose slowly at the appointed moment, and reached the height of the treetops; they made a live, sonorous noise that mingled magically with the music. I had never dared dream of anything like it. Unfortunately, we could not achieve the same effect in Monte Carlo (Waltz was no longer with us) nor at the Costanzi, in Rome, nor at Covent Garden, in London. (In London, my ballet, danced by the Diaghilev company, was honored by being included in the gala performance on the occasion of the coronation ceremonies of 1911.)

When Diaghilev took over the Châtelet, he found that the theatre, which dated back to the time of Napoleon III, did not suit—in elegance or even in cleanliness—the splendor of the artistic feast he was about to offer Paris. He decided, therefore, to go to extraordinary expense to give it a more brilliant appearance. He had the auditorium, the two foyers, and the loges cleaned and, in places, repainted, and—this was real madness—had the aisles carpeted in a ruby-red upholstery. That's the kind of man Serge was. For all my protests on grounds of common sense and economy, I could not help but admire the boldness of his exuberant temperament, which had all the virtues and all the faults typical of Russians. In general, Diaghilev's seductive charm for all who came in contact with him grew precisely from such excesses of folly.

Everything happened for the best. Our sense of well-deserved success filled us with happiness. I will never forget our night walk—Serge's and mine —after the supper he had given for a group of our fellow artists following the dress rehearsal, on which occasion Gabriel Astruc had assembled an odd mixture of the most prominent representatives of the fashionable world and the demimonde of Paris. Our wandering through the streets and squares of Paris lasted until dawn, drunk as we were on extraordinary amounts of champagne and the emotions we had just experienced. And without delay, we fell to planning all kinds of projects, each more daring than the last. The prospect of the next day's extremely disagreeable conversations with creditors and suppliers did not greatly worry Diaghilev; a large part of our purchases (the ruby-red carpeting, etc.) had been on credit, and there were a lot of other expenses still to be settled, whereas box-office receipts barely sufficed to pay the two companies (opera and ballet). The situation was eased somewhat by the financial assistance of a few compatriots and by French friends whose support we had won with *Boris Godunov*. Several painters and poets had been conquered once and for all by Diaghilev, and while he remained for us the same Serge, that night he stepped forth on the world stage and began his triumphal progress under the name of Serge Diaghilev.

When we drew up the balance sheet for the first opera and ballet season in Paris, in 1909, we had to face the fact that ballet had taken the lead over opera, and this despite the presence of Chalia-pin, Litvinne, Kastorsky, and many other excellent artists; despite unparalleled orchestral conductors —Tcherepnine and Cooper; and despite the magnificence of the staging. Serov's *Judith* and Glinka's Prologue to *Russlan* went almost unnoticed and unreviewed except for quite brief *succès d'estime* comments in the press. Only the one act of Borodin's *Prince Igor* had met with resounding success, but there again it was not the operatic but the balletic element that had generated enthusiasm. Looking to the future, Diaghilev saw himself, quite contrary to his own taste, forced to limit his Parisian repertoire to ballets, and having to relinquish the operas. Nonetheless, he tried to come back to opera several times with splendid productions of Moussorgsky's *Khovanshchina*, Stravinsky's *Le Rossignol* (the first operatic version dates from 1914), and Rimsky-Korsakov's *Le Coq d'Or*. Much later, Diaghilev presented some comic operas by Gounod, *Le Astuzie Femminili* by Cimarosa, and *L'Éducation Manquée* by Chabrier.

In 1914, we presented *Le Coq d'Or* in a special production of my devising in which all the action was presented as ballet (mime and dance), with the singing (chorus and principal singing roles) relegated to the status of a vocal accompaniment. The reason for such a heresy was the mis-matching, which too often becomes disturbing in opera, of unattractive heroes and heroines: an Isolde whom Tristan can scarcely enfold in his arms; a pot-bellied, bandy-legged Faust paying court to a massive Marguerite. The ballet excludes such visual monstrosities. In its new aspect and thanks to the choreographic taste of Fokine and the glowing colors of the décor and costumes by Mme. Gontcharova, *Le Coq d'Or* was received with enthusiasm. It was an isolated bit of audacity, however, and when I myself restaged this work, of which I am particularly fond (at the Paris Opéra, in 1927), I no longer dared revert to my old paradox.

It is curious to note that Diaghilev presented nothing by Tchaikovsky, either in 1909 or later, although he worshiped this composer as much as did our entire group. This man who was bold to the point of temerity, this fearless, blameless knight, did not dare run counter to French music criticism and its ineradicable prejudice which decreed, once and for all, that Tchaikovsky was not an original musician incarnating the spirit of his people, that he was not "sufficiently Russian." It was not until 1922 that Diaghilev resolved to present *The Sleeping Beauty* in London; unfortunately, it did not meet with sufficient success to cover the costs of its grandiose production, and only one act, under the title of *Aurora's Wedding*, was included in the permanent repertoire of the Ballets Russes. Even then, Serge held back from presenting it in a special mise-en-scène; he borrowed the old, worn costumes of *Le Pavillon d'Armide*, which had been produced twenty years earlier.

Thus it was that opera gave way to ballet. Fokine, by the poetry or grace or brilliance or vigor of his inventiveness, amazed and charmed the French public in a fashion that was altogether unusual in Western Europe and rare even in Russia. Furthermore, Fokine was not only the innovator of certain ballet forms; he also created an entirely new spirit in his performers. It is unlikely that even he could have succeeded in his reform without such talented dancers, who were consummate masters of their art and whose technical training was analogous to his own.

Among the artistic personalities who stood out from the group, foremost was Vaslav Nijinsky—the new "god of the dance," an incarnate miracle of choreographic art whose meteoric career ended at the very moment when one looked to him for so many fresh prodigies. Nijinsky became the instant focus of public interest. His appearance onstage aroused unflagging, ardent, avid attention, culminating in thunderous ovations. Unfortunately, Diaghilev considered this was not enough; in his extreme predilection for the young artist, he was not satisfied to give him the chance to triumph as a performer only, but wanted to make him a great creator of ballets. By showing too conspicuous a preference for Nijinsky—to the detriment especially of Fokine and the other first-rank artists—Diaghilev created a coolness in his relations with them; presently, envy and self-interest replaced the friendship and mutual esteem with which our collaboration had begun. It was such feelings that subsequently led Fokine to insist on terms that heavily burdened the company's budget and in the end became impossible. On the other hand, Nijinsky's activities as ballet master did not, in my opinion, produce happy results. It is true that a great scandal was precipitated by the audacity of the gestures and positions in *L'Après-Midi d'un Faune*. In *Le Sacre du Printemps* Nijinsky compelled the dancers to contort themselves in the most grotesque poses, intended to represent the condition of slaves in antiquity. This enraptured the ranks of the aesthetes and snobs, and Diaghilev could rejoice, flattered by having been assigned the lofty role of marching at the head of the most rarefied Parisian avant-garde. But can one compare these works, so studied and forced, to the free inspiration, so attuned to the music, which Fokine and Romanov and, later, Massine and Mme. Nijinska revealed in creating ensembles that were truly poetic and intensely appealing?

———————————

I should like to dwell for a moment on Nijinsky's first appearance on the stage in Paris. His appearance elicited from the public an "Ah!" that expressed *genuine* delight. Nijinsky was still dancing the role of the Favorite Slave in *Armide*, but his dance no longer opened with the famous prodigious standing leap. It began with a deliciously graceful pas de trois, danced with rare perfection by Nijinsky and Mmes. Fedorova and Karsavina. This number had been substituted for the "Evocation of the Shades," which slowed the action too much. At first, I regretted the elimination of this very Hoffmannesque passage, but I had to concede that the new dance, this pas de trois, performed to the delicate, tenderly melancholy music of the "Shades," had so evocative a quality, was such a happy find, that I was readily consoled. For the new number, I had designed an ensemble of three costumes that stood out effectively against the dark foliage of the enchanted garden. Nijinsky was dressed *alla turca* in a costume of silver cloth with a touch of yellow and a bit of ermine; his two partners wore bright yellow, with gold embroideries. The appearance of the group, Nijinsky's classical gesture of arm upraised, his impeccable entrechats, his way of seeming to float on air, accompanied by the curtsies of his partners, created a fairy-like vision. I believe that nothing like it had been seen since the days of Noverre and Didelot.

And what can one say of Nijinsky in *Les Sylphides*! Here was a vision dreamed by the Romantics in the era of Taglioni, Grisi, and Petipa. . . . Vaulting, soaring leaps—one had the impression of an unreal, weightless being, a spirit. . . . Watching Nijinsky move, one could not believe he was subject to the law of gravity, nor think that his breathing had to be rigidly controlled, that his movements required great effort. What was the man's secret? Where could this Russian-Polish boy, at that time utterly without any experience of life, have drawn his understanding of so refined an art? Subsequently we had the opportunity to admire Nijinsky in *Schéhérazade* and, above all, in *Petrouchka*, where he astounded us by the tragic nuances he brought to his role. Yet the first appearance of Nijinsky on the Paris stage lives in my memory as a vision of "absolute beauty."

Similarly, Tamara Karsavina was one of our most important acquisitions, starting with our first Paris season, and for years thereafter she was our prima ballerina. The success of our performances depended in large part on her. After she left the Imperial School, Tamara Platonovna

Karsavina, whose father was a retired dancer, had attracted wide attention because of her appealing beauty. Fokine, however, accused her of being lazy, obtuse, and not serious enough. Just possibly this was said out of lover's spite since his proposals of marriage had been pitilessly refused by the young artist. Pavlova's absence at the opening of the season had obliged Diaghilev to approach Karalli first for the role of Armide, but when Karalli had to leave for another engagement, we were able to persuade Fokine to entrust the role to Karsavina, who had had time to study it thoroughly by watching her fellow artists perform. The experiment was absolutely conclusive. Henceforth, one could place complete confidence in her; even if Fokine's strictures had been justified a few years earlier, there remained in her not the slightest trace of laziness or insouciance.

Thereafter Karsavina set an example of thoughtful work by an artist who was entirely and conscientiously aware of her responsibility. This charming young woman, who had an adorable, resounding, childlike laugh, displayed an exceptional seriousness about her art. She loved to read, and not only Russian books. She had an equal passion for painting and music, and in general, while utterly free of pedantry, was far more cultivated than any of her friends and companions. Actually, she did not have *friends*; she held herself a bit aloof and did not share in group amusements. With her innate tact and her cultivated refinement, Karsavina truly represented an *ideal* from every point of view, and there was nothing surprising in her advancement and success. Diaghilev could be sure that Karsavina would not betray him and would not create difficulties for him. She never made exaggerated demands and, provided her rights were not too much encroached upon, she was agreeable to all the concessions asked of her, her passion for her art taking precedence over all else. Her excellent character, her candor and goodness meant that later she was often exploited by our tyrannical leader, but on the whole the years went by without the slightest misunderstanding between them. She was a veritable treasure, and only external circumstances—the same as those that separated me from our work in common—prevented her after the First World War from remaining the good fairy of the Ballets Russes.

Space does not allow me to mention all the interesting members of our numerous company, which included so many delightful artists. Yet how can one not mention the two Fedorova sisters, Sophia and Olga (Sophia was very popular in Moscow and for a long time was prima ballerina of the Imperial Ballet), or the gracious and charming Yelena Smirnova, or Bronislava Nijinska, the sister of Vaslav Nijinsky, who proved later to be a metteur-en-scène of the first order. And among the men, Bolm, the unforgettable Chief Warrior in the *Polovetsian Dances*, who elicited frantic bravos; or Orlov, with his very provocative talent in the grotesque genre. Then there were Zverev, Froman, Obukhov, Kremnev, Bulgakov—and, last, the corps de ballet, which, for all its admirable discipline, had nothing whatever mechanical about its movements. In our troupe the very last soldier was aware of his duty, and the ensemble testified to this, being remarkably harmonious and ordered, without any suggestion of rigidity. For years this indissolubly united ensemble held together, even in the midst of political catastrophes that shook the whole world.

By way of conclusion, would it not perhaps be useful to state precisely what the famous Ballets Russes really did represent? The public, both in Europe and in America, tended to think of them as the touring company of the Imperial Russian Ballet, which was celebrated far beyond our country's borders. But despite the fact that Diaghilev's entire company came from the Maryinsky Theatre in St. Petersburg and the Grand Theatre in Moscow, this theory has no validity, for all the musical, choreographic, and other production elements of his ballet programs were conceived afresh—especially for the Paris season. In Russia, on the other hand, there were well-established ballet-omanes, critics, and artists (the latter vexed at not having been invited to join our enterprise) who spoke only ill of us and claimed that unworthy amateurs were daring to dishonor Russian art abroad by producing God knew what grotesque spectacles in the worst possible taste.

There's no denying it—we really were a "company of usurpers"! However, far from being amateurs unfamiliar with ballet, the leading members of our group had dreamed from childhood of devoting their talents to the glory of Terpsichore. As for me—and I can consider myself the instigator and originator of the whole enterprise—my passion for ballet was born when, at the age of seven, I saw my first ballet performance, which was *La Bayadère*. From then on, its appeal grew only greater, and my enthusiasm became more and more informed. The stages of this evolution were the productions of *Coppélia* and *Giselle* in 1884, the arrival in 1885 of the "divine" Virginia Zucchi, and, finally, in 1890, the enchantment of *The Sleeping Beauty*. The first friends won over to my cause were Walter Nouvel and D. V. Filosofov; and then there came to join us Filosofov's "country cousin"—Diaghilev—and the Beaux-Arts student L. S. Rosenberg-Bakst. The five of us took the preliminary steps toward founding the famous Ballets Russes, and we remained its leaders, together with the musicians Tcherepnine and Stravinsky (and later Prokofiev) and the ballet specialists Fokine, Romanov, Nijinsky, Massine, and, later, Nijinska, Balanchine, Lifar, and Kochno.

———————

I spoke earlier of the role Diaghilev's forced resignation in 1901 played in his career. It marked the end of his activity in the Imperial Theatres. Now, in those days it was impossible to establish workable ballet enterprises in competition with the state theatres. No one could have recruited the necessary performers, since no dance schools other than the Imperial School existed. Accordingly, we dreamed of forming our own company on the basis of what already existed, and gradually these dreams led us to the "export campaign." Furthermore, while we loved and admired our Imperial Ballet, we were eager to renew and rejuvenate it, but this became impossible with the advent of Telyakovsky. The production of *Le Pavillon d'Armide* and its success were decisive in realizing our hopes. Preparing for this ballet brought first me, and then all our group, in contact with Fokine, and it so happened that this excellent artist entirely shared our tastes and asked for nothing better than to perfect his art through contact with his new friends. Naturally, Fokine's extraordinary talent would have manifested itself alone, but it is also undeniable that he would never have made such a brilliant and impressive debut in 1909 had he remained in his earlier milieu. The fresh air he breathed thanks to his contact with the *World of Art* group inspired him and pushed him toward experimentation. On the other hand, the best intentions of the originators would have come to nothing had Diaghilev not crossed our path— Diaghilev, with his talent for handling people, his great business acumen, and, what was precious above all else, his fanatical idealism and his disinterestedness.

In 1909, Paris saw something *especially created for her*, something that could have existed nowhere else. The artists brought to Paris in Diaghilev's company were Russian, naturally, but when they found themselves on new terrain they acquired a new self-awareness, and this is what gave them fresh strength and the means to compel unqualified recognition. Actually, in an art as notably universal as ballet, it would be unfair to trace everything back to narrowly national boundaries. Would it not be fairer to think of the Ballets Russes, which so stirred and overwhelmed European society, as the return to a shared homeland of an art that had been born earlier in Italy, in France, in Germany, and that during its long sojourn on the banks of the Neva, in the capital of the Russian Empire, miraculously preserved an unfailing freshness?

Paris, March–August, 1944

Alexandre Benois, by Bakst, 1895

AUTHOR'S NOTE

I did not have the good fortune to be present at the beginning of Serge de Diaghilev's Ballets Russes. For the annotations in the early pages of these reminiscences and for the captions of photographs of ballets produced prior to my taking part in the work of the company, I have relied on what Diaghilev himself has reported and on the testimony of his first collaborators and the friends of his youth.

Pavlova in *Les Sylphides*; program by Valentin Serov

LE
PAVILLON D'ARMIDE

Ballet in three scenes by Alexandre Benois, based on a short story by Théophile Gautier. Music by Nicholas Tcherepnine. Choreography by Michel Fokine. Décor and costumes by Benois. First performance in Paris: Théâtre du Châtelet, May 19, 1909.

L*e Pavillon d'Armide* was first performed at the Maryinsky Theatre, in St. Petersburg, on November 25, 1907.

Benois and Tcherepnine had begun work on this ballet in 1901–2, and the first choreographic version of the second scene, the "Dream Scene," was created by Fokine in the spring of 1907 for the graduation exercises at the St. Petersburg Imperial School of Ballet.

That same year, Tcherepnine completed the music for the first and third scenes, and put his score into final form.

The production of *Le Pavillon* at the Maryinsky Theatre was beset by administrative complications and upsets. Mathilda Kchessinska, who was to dance Armide, refused to dance the part a few days before the première and was replaced by Anna Pavlova.

At the Paris dress rehearsal, on May 18, 1909, the principal roles were danced by Vera Karalli and Mikhail Mordkin, stars of the Imperial Theatre of Moscow; on May 19, at the opening-night performance, by Pavlova and Fokine. In subsequent Diaghilev productions, the interpreters of these roles were Tamara Karsavina, who earlier had danced one of the Confidantes, and Adolph Bolm. Vaslav Nijinsky made his triumphal Paris debut at the dress rehearsal of *Pavillon*, dancing the role of the Slave.

Benois set for Scene II, *Le Pavillon d'Armide*

POLOVETSIAN DANCES FROM PRINCE IGOR

Music by Alexander Borodin. Choreography by Michel Fokine. Curtain, décor, and costumes by Nicholas Roerich. First performance: Théâtre du Châtelet, Paris, May 19, 1909.

During the first Paris season of the Ballets Russes, in 1909, dance programs were alternated with operas, among them *Prince Igor*. Serge Grigoriev, who was Diaghilev's regisseur for twenty years (1909–29), wrote of the preparations for this season: "Diaghilev's chief interest was centered on the opera, the performances of which were to be the main event of the season; the ballet was no more than an extra."

However, the importance of the choreographed portion of the third act of *Prince Igor*, in which the principal roles were danced by Sophia Fedorova, Yelena Smirnova, and Adolph Bolm, made Diaghilev decide to include this fragment in his program of ballets.

The very first rehearsal of the ballet company he had organized, which took place on April 2, 1909, at the Salle Catherine, in St. Petersburg, was devoted to working out the choreography for the *Polovetsian Dances* that Fokine created for the Ballets Russes.

LE FESTIN

A suite of dances. Décor by Constantine Korovine. Costumes by Bakst, Benois, Bilibine, and Korovine. First performance: Théâtre du Châtelet, Paris, May 19, 1909.

Alexis Koslov
and Alexandra Baldina

Diaghilev had no time to prepare a third new ballet for the opening performance of his first Paris season, and he therefore completed the program with *Le Festin*, a divertissement composed of dances taken from operas and ballets in the repertoires of the Maryinsky Theatre and the Grand Theatre of Moscow.

The only new choreography in *Le Festin* was the "Finale," which Michel Fokine staged for the corps de ballet, using the last movement of Tchaikovsky's Symphony No. 2, in which the composer developed the musical theme of the Ukrainian dance "the stork." For scenery, Diaghilev borrowed the set used in the first scene of Glinka's opera *Russlan and Ludmila*, which he was presenting that season also. He had new costumes made for the dancers after sketches by young Russian painters.

Le Festin included the following numbers:

(1) "Cortege" (march from Rimsky-Korsakov's *Le Coq d'Or*).

(2) "Lezghinka" (from Glinka's opera *Russlan and Ludmila*). Choreography by Marius Petipa and Fokine.
Vera Fokina and ten male dancers from the corps de ballet.

(3) "Fire Bird" ("The Blue Bird and the Enchanted Princess" pas de deux from Tchaikovsky's ballet *The Sleeping Beauty*). Choreography by Petipa.
Tamara Karsavina and Vaslav Nijinsky.
(This pas de deux, under the title "The Golden Bird," was repeated with the same dancers in the Ballets Russes's season at the Vienna Opera in January, 1913.)

(4) "Czardas" (from Glazounov's ballet *Raymonda*). Choreography by Alexander Gorsky.
Sophia Fedorova and Mikhail Mordkin.

(5) "Hopak" (from Moussorgsky's opera *The Fair at Sorochinsk*). Choreography by Fokine.
Olga Fedorova, Nicholas Kremnev, and eight male and female dancers from the corps de ballet.

(6) "Mazurka" (from Glinka's opera *A Life for the Czar*). Choreography by Nicholas Goltz and Felix Kchessinsky.
Eight male and female dancers from the corps de ballet.

(7) "Trepak" (from Tchaikovsky's ballet *The Nutcracker*). Choreography by Fokine.

(8) "Grand Pas Classique Hongrois" (from Glazounov's ballet *Raymonda*). Choreography by Petipa.
Vera Karalli, Mikhail Mordkin, and an ensemble of sixteen dancers, among them Vaslav Nijinsky, Adolph Bolm, Laurent Novikov, Alexis Koslov, Bronislava Nijinska, Alexandra Baldina, Ludmila Schollar, Yelena Smirnova.

(9) "Finale" (music from Tchaikovsky's Symphony No. 2). Choreography by Fokine.
Ensemble of the corps de ballet.

Nijinsky in "Fire Bird," *Le Festin*

Some twenty years after the first Paris appearance of the Ballets Russes, Countess Anna de Noailles wrote a "Farewell to the Ballets Russes," which appeared in the *Revue Musicale* on December 1, 1930. She said, in part:

No one thought that in the realm of art there might be something utterly new under the sun when, in instant splendor, there appeared the phenomenon of the Ballets Russes.

In the spring of 1909, every capital of Europe had a Ballets Russes première. I attended the one in Paris. It was as if the creation of the world had added something to its seventh day. When I entered the loge to which I had been invited—and I arrived a little late, for I had not believed the several initiates who promised me a revelation—I understood that I was witnessing a miracle. I was seeing something that had never before existed. Everything that dazzles, intoxicates and seduces us had been conjured up and drawn onto the stage, there to flower as naturally, as perfectly as the plant world attains its magnificence under the influence of the climate.

LES SYLPHIDES

A romantic reverie in one act by Michel Fokine. Music by Frédéric Chopin, seven piano pieces orchestrated for the Ballets Russes production by Sergei Taneyev, Anatole Liadov, Alexander Glazounov, Nicholas Tcherepnine, and Igor Stravinsky. Choreography by Michel Fokine. Décor and costumes by Alexandre Benois. (In 1917, a new set by Carlo Sokrate replaced the Benois décor.) First performance by the Ballets Russes: Théâtre du Châtelet, Paris, June 2, 1909. Principal dancers: Anna Pavlova, Tamara Karsavina, Alexandra Baldina, Vaslav Nijinsky.

The first version of this ballet, entitled *Chopiniana*, was created for a benefit performance at the Maryinsky Theatre, in St. Petersburg, on February 10, 1907. For this production, the orchestration was by Glazounov. The mise-en-scène was borrowed from the Maryinsky's stock: white tutus "à la Taglioni," and a section of the backdrop for the third scene of *Sleeping Beauty*, painted in 1890 by the stage designer M. I. Botcharov. However, for "The Waltz," new costumes were made after sketches by Léon Bakst.

The same version, retitled *Dances to Music by Chopin*, was presented at a benefit performance at the Maryinsky on March 8, 1908.

A new version, entitled *Grand Pas to Music by Chopin* and orchestrated by Glazounov and Maurice Keller, was offered at the graduation exercises of the Imperial Ballet School of St. Petersburg, held at the Maryinsky on February 19, 1909.

CLEOPATRE

Choreographic drama in one act. Music by Anton Arensky and Sergei Taneyev, Nicholas Rimsky-Korsakov, Mikhail Glinka, Modest Moussorgsky, Alexander Glazounov, Nicholas Tcherepnine. Staging and choreography by Michel Fokine. Décor, costumes, and props after drawings by Léon Bakst. First performance: Théâtre du Châtelet, Paris, June 2, 1909.

The first version of *Cléopâtre* was presented under the title *Nuit d'Égypte* on March 8, 1908, as part of a benefit at the Maryinsky Theatre, in St. Petersburg. On this occasion, the music of the ballet, which Fokine had choreographed, included only Arensky's score. Most of the costumes were borrowed from *La Fille du Pharaon* and *Aïda*, although several new costumes for the soloists were made after sketches by Bakst. For the set, a background drop from one of the operas in the repertoire was retouched by the Maryinsky's stage designer, Oreste Allegri.

For the Paris season, Diaghilev ordered a new mise-en-scène from Bakst and, on the advice of Alexandre Benois, added to the Arensky score symphonic excerpts by several other Russian composers; also, he replaced the "happy ending" of *Nuit d'Égypte* with a dramatic pantomime.

Ida Rubinstein, then a young nonprofessional who was studying with Fokine, made her first stage appearance in *Cléopâtre*. She was to have appeared earlier in Oscar Wilde's poetic drama *Salomé*—Fokine had created Salomé's dance to music by Glazounov, and Rubinstein's costume had been designed by Bakst—but after the dress rehearsal in St. Petersburg, the play was suppressed by the censor.

In 1913, Jean Cocteau described Rubinstein's entrance thus:

The ballet is too famous and M. Bakst's sets and costumes too noteworthy for my comments to contribute to them in any way, but the unforgettable entrance of Mme. Ida Rubinstein must be recorded for all time. I shall merely transcribe a few notes I jotted down in the course of early performances. May that feeling of immediacy, which memory cannot recapture, excuse their disorder. . . .

Then a ritual cortege was seen to appear. There were musicians who plucked long, oval-shaped citharas, their tones richly resonant yet as soft as the breathing of serpents. Flutists, their arms raised in angular poses, blew from their sonorous pipes spirals of sound so piercing, so sharp, ascending and descending in turn, that one's nerves could hardly endure them. There were terra-cotta-complexioned fauns, with long white manes; narrow-hipped young women with pointed elbows and flat eyes; and all the other attendants on a royal galley.

Finally, borne on the shoulders of six colossi, there appeared a kind of ebony and gold casket, which a young black watched over diligently, touching it, clearing the way for it, urging on the bearers.

The bearers set the casket down in the middle of the temple, opened its double lid, and from within lifted a kind of mummy, a bundle of veils, which they placed upright on its ivory pattens. Then four slaves began an astonishing maneuver. They unwound the first veil, which was red, with silver lotuses and crocodiles; then the second veil, which was green with the history of the dynasties in gold filigree; then the third, which was orange with prismatic stripes; and so on until the twelfth veil, a dark blue, which, one divined, enclosed the body of a woman. Each veil was unwound in a different fashion: one called for a manège of intricately patterned steps, another for the skill needed to shell a ripe nut, another for the casualness with which one plucks the petals of a rose; the eleventh veil, in what seemed the most difficult movement, was peeled off in one piece like the bark of a eucalyptus.

The twelfth veil, dark blue, Mme. Rubinstein released herself, letting it fall with a sweeping, circular gesture.

Bakst and Diaghilev

Karsavina in *Cléopâtre*

She stood leaning forward, her shoulders slightly humped like the wings of the ibis; overcome by her long wait, having submitted in her dark coffin, as had we, to the intolerable and sublime music of her cortege, she wavered on her high pattens. She was wearing a small blue wig, from which a short golden braid hung down on either side of her face. There she stood, unswathed, eyes vacant, cheeks pale, lips parted, shoulders hunched, and as she confronted the stunned audience, she was too beautiful, like a too potent Oriental fragrance.

In his *Reminiscences of the Ballets Russes,* Alexandre Benois claims credit for the idea for this entrance, although generally its paternity is attributed to Bakst.

The fresh aspect Bakst gave Egyptian antiquity in *Cléopâtre* seemed, at the time the ballet was created, like a surprising discovery in the field of archaeology. Diaghilev told me that Kaiser Wilhelm II, after having attended the opening night of *Cléopâtre* in Berlin, had called together the members of a society of Egyptologists of which he was president to talk to them about the cultural significance of the ballet and to urge them to study Bakst's mise-en-scène.

In 1917, during the Ballets Russes tour in Latin America, the set for *Cléopâtre* was destroyed by fire; in July, 1918, Diaghilev ordered a new décor from Robert Delaunay, and, from his wife, Sonia, sketches for new costumes for Lubov Tchernicheva and Leonide Massine, who were dancing the roles created by Rubinstein and Fokine.

LE
CARNAVAL

Pantomime ballet in one act by Michel Fokine. Music by Robert Schumann, orchestrated by Nicholas Rimsky-Korsakov, Anatole Liadov, Nicholas Tcherepnine, and Alexander Glazounov. Choreography by Fokine. Décor and costumes by Léon Bakst. First performance by the Ballets Russes: Teater des Westens, Berlin, May 20, 1910. First performance in Paris: Théâtre National de l'Opéra, June 4, 1910.

Fokine had created *Carnaval* for a benefit given in St. Petersburg on February 20, 1910. In May of the same year, the ballet was included in the repertoire of the Ballets Russes.

The first sketch for the *Carnaval* set which Bakst submitted to Diaghilev represented an immense terrace overlooking a garden, but for this particular ballet Diaghilev wanted to circumscribe the stage area at the Opéra, and he suggested to Bakst the idea of an interior.

The success of *Carnaval* in Paris was due, in large part, to the brilliant execution of Fokine's choreography by Karsavina and Nijinsky.

In his *Notes on the Ballet*, Jean Cocteau described Nijinsky in *Carnaval*:

What does call for comment is M. Nijinsky's Harlequin. A kind of middle-class Hermes, an acrobatic cat stuffed full of candid lechery and crafty indifference, a schoolboy (notice the

collar and necktie in the Bakst water color), wheedling, thieving,
swift-footed, utterly freed of the chains of gravity, a creature of
perfect mathematical grace.

Desire, mischief, self-satisfaction, arrogance, rapid bob-
bings of his head, and still other things, but especially a way of
peering out from under the visor of the cap he wore pulled down
over his eyebrows, the way one shoulder was raised higher than
the other and his cheek pressed against it, the way the right hand
was outstretched, the leg poised to relax, such—and it was some-
thing never before granted me to see or hear at the theatre—such
was Vaslav Nijinsky in Carnaval, *surrounded by an uninterrupt-*
ed roar of applause.

Diaghilev told me about a funny incident that occurred
during one performance of *Le Carnaval*. Enrico Cecchetti, who
was miming the role of Pantalon, an elderly dandy of the
Romantic period, mixed up the order of the program one evening and appeared onstage in *Carnaval* dressed in his costume
for the Chief Eunuch in *Schéhérazade*.

Nijinsky in
Schéhérazade, sketch by
Jean Cocteau

Diaghilev
and Nijinsky, sketch by
Jean Cocteau

SCHEHERAZADE

Choreographic drama in one act by Léon Bakst and Michel Fokine. Music by Nicholas Rimsky-Korsakov. Choreography by Fokine. Décor and costumes by Bakst. First performance: Théâtre National de l'Opéra, Paris, June 4, 1910.

Schéhérazade was the first true creation of the Ballets Russes, because, except for the dances from the opera *Prince Igor* that Fokine had choreographed for the company in 1909, all the other ballets in Diaghilev's first Paris season were fresh versions of already existing works.

The libretto for *Schéhérazade* was signed with Bakst's name, but Alexandre Benois informs us in his *Memoirs* that he was its author; he had been the first to think of adapting Rimsky-Korsakov's symphonic poem for the stage, he writes, and he had conceived its theatrical presentation. But when, affronted by the omission of his name from the program, he asked for an explanation, Diaghilev answered, "What do you expect! Bakst had to be given something. You have *Le Pavillon d'Armide*, he's got *Schéhérazade*!"

In the autumn of 1910, Diaghilev ordered a proscenium curtain for the ballet from Valentin Serov, who had designed the first Ballets Russes poster. Inspired by Persian miniatures, the curtain was completed by Serov in Paris, in 1911, and figured in the ballet's performances until 1914, when it was lost in the warehouse where the Ballets Russes props were stored.

Bakst sketch for *Schéhérazade*

Fokine and Fokina
in *Schéhérazade*

———

Ida Rubinstein,
by Jacques-Émile Blanche

———

Ida Rubinstein in
Schéhérazade

(Top) Bulgakov;
(bottom) Kissilev in
Schéhérazade

———

Schéhérazade,
set and
costumes by Bakst

Schéhérazade was a total success thanks to the harmonious combination of music, mise-en-scène, and choreography. Bakst's décor and costumes turned theatrical concepts of the period upside down, and engendered the so-called "Ballets Russes style." The miming of Ida Rubinstein, Nijinsky's dances, and the ensembles devised by Fokine aroused a degree of interest that was unusual for a dance performance; quite simply, they created a sensation.

Such enthusiasm persuaded Sarah Bernhardt to see the ballet. Already lame, the great tragedienne had herself carried into the theatre, but scarcely had the curtain gone up than she was seen to become much overwrought. Laying about her with her cane, she cried, "Let's get out of here! Quickly! . . . I'm afraid. They are all mutes!"

Nijinsky
in the first act of *Giselle*

Scherer and
Ognev in *Giselle*

Karsavina
in the first act of *Giselle*

(Overleaf) Karsavina
and Nijinsky in the second
act of *Giselle*

GISELLE

Pantomime ballet in two acts by Vernoy de Saint-Georges, Théophile Gautier, and Jean Coralli. Music by Adolphe Adam. Décor and costumes by Alexandre Benois. First performance by the Ballets Russes: Théâtre National de l'Opéra, Paris, June 18, 1910.

The traditional style of Benois's décor for *Giselle* disappointed Parisian audiences and misled them into thinking that the sets came from some of the Opéra's old stock. Also, this romantic ballet, which had been in the repertoire of the Théâtre National for almost a century, seemed out of place among Diaghilev's revolutionary productions, and it enjoyed no more than a *succès d'estime*.

Only Karsavina and Nijinsky were acclaimed by the admirers of classical ballet. Nijinsky surpassed himself in the airborne leaps of the second scene, but in the dramatic moments his playing lacked expression, and in the scene in which Giselle goes mad he moved away from the center of the action and stood motionless. When Diaghilev mentioned this to him, Nijinsky replied, "I'm acting with my eyes!"

FIREBIRD

Folk tale in two scenes by Michel Fokine. Music by Igor Stravinsky. Choreography by Fokine. Décor by Alexander Golovine. Costumes for Tamara Karsavina and Fokine by Léon Bakst. First performance: Théâtre National de l'Opéra, Paris, June 25, 1910.

Despite the advice of friends that he commission the score for *Firebird* from Sergei Vassilenko, who had composed several ballets produced in Russia but who was little known in Europe, Diaghilev first approached Anatole Liadov. Then he heard a concert performance of *Fireworks* and *Scherzo Fantastique*, and was so enthusiastic that he changed his mind and asked Stravinsky to write the score for the new ballet.

Diaghilev embarked on the production of *Firebird* because he expected Anna Pavlova to appear in his 1910 Paris season, and he intended the principal role in the ballet for her. But Pavlova found Stravinsky's music incomprehensible and refused to dance the Firebird.

When Nijinsky heard that Pavlova had withdrawn, he asked Diaghilev to entrust the role to him. To lend plausibility to his request, Nijinsky cited the example of Petipa's pas de deux, "The Blue Bird and the Enchanted Princess," in which the role of the Bird is interpreted by a male dancer. Nijinsky also wanted to dance the Firebird on point. (Later, in the second scene of *Petrouchka*, he did dance on point from time to time.)

For all of Nijinsky's insistence, in the end the role of the Firebird was created by Karsavina, who, before Pavlova's withdrawal, had been assigned by Diaghilev to the role of the Czarevna.

In 1921, Bakst submitted a proposal to Diaghilev for a new mise-en-scène for *Firebird*. He envisaged the ballet as a kingdom of flying creatures, for which the décor would be a gigantic nest; Kostchei he visualized as an owl.

However, it was only in 1926 that Diaghilev decided to revamp Golovine's by then shabby sets and costumes, and he ordered new sketches from Nathalie Gontcharova. He took an active part in working out this new version, and on August 7, 1926, wrote to me from Venice:

Serge Grigoriev

One further commission, and the most important. *Gontcharova must be commissioned to prepare the mise-en-scène for* Firebird. *It is hard to discuss this with her by letter. On your way here, could you not come by way of Juan-les-Pins and see them [Gontcharova and her husband, Michel Larionov] and explain my ideas to them.*

First scene: A dark night, with phosphorescent apples. The stage is full of apples, and not a single tree; the garden [orchard] is dark brown. The décor must be worked out in minute detail—like Mantegna's "hunt" in Mantua, or like the Avignon frescoes. Then, for the second scene the back cloth is changed: the garden is transformed into the Holy City, the apples become the gilded onion domes of churches, a countless swarm of churches crowded together.

Gontcharova followed Diaghilev's indications to the letter, only eliminating, with his consent, the phosphorescence.

In the revival of *Firebird* with its new sets, George Balanchine mimed the role of the immortal Kostchei. His capers often won him sharp reprimands from Diaghilev, because some evenings, in interpreting this evil genie whom Fokine's scenario describes as a "foul, green-fingered giant who terrorized travelers and held them prisoners within his un-yielding walls," Balanchine would make him a hilarious character and send the audience into gales of laughter with his pranks.

In 1917, at the Théâtre du Châtelet, in Paris, Diaghilev introduced an innovation into the performance that Serge Grigoriev, in his book, *The Diaghilev Ballet: 1909–1929*, described thus:

We were to give our first performance on 11 May with L'Oiseau de Feu *in the programme, and a day or two before it Diaghilev announced that he had decided to make an alteration in the final tableau of that ballet to accord with the spirit of the times. Instead of being presented with a crown and sceptre, as he had been hitherto, the Tsarevich would in future receive a cap of Liberty and a red flag. This was by way of homage to the first, the "Liberal," Russian Revolution of February 1917. For at that time, though he professed himself a Monarchist, Diaghilev favoured the recent change of régime and wished to pay it tribute. His idea was that the red flag would symbolize a victory of the forces of light over those of darkness, represented by Koshchey.*

The Paris public accorded this symbolic episode a glacial reception, and Diaghilev received numerous letters of protest, which led him to reinstate the original version of the ballet's finale.

LES
ORIENTALES

Choreographic sketches. Music by Alexander Glazounov, Christian Sinding, Anton Arensky, Edvard Grieg, Alexander Borodin. Décor by Constantine Korovine. First performance: Théâtre National de l'Opéra, Paris, June 25, 1910.

For the second season of the Ballets Russes in Paris, Diaghilev replaced *Le Festin* with a new suite of dances, *Les Orientales*. In this divertissement, Nijinsky appeared twice, in dances choreographed by himself—"La Danse Siamoise," to music by Sinding, and a "Variation," to music by Grieg that Stravinsky orchestrated.

The other soloists in *Les Orientales* were Tamara Karsavina, Vasily Geltzer, Vera Fokina, Alexander Volinine, and Alexander Orlov.

LE
SPECTRE DE LA ROSE

Ballet in one scene, after a poem by Théophile Gautier, adapted by Jean-Louis Vaudoyer. Music by Carl Maria von Weber, orchestrated by Hector Berlioz. Choreography by Michel Fokine. Décor and costumes by Léon Bakst. First performance: Casino, Monte Carlo, April 19, 1911.

Soulève ta paupière close

Qu'effleure un songe virginal;

Je suis le spectre de la rose

Que tu portais hier au bal.

The idea of adapting Weber's "Invitation to the Dance" for the stage came to Diaghilev one day while talking with Nijinsky, and eventually he asked Vaudoyer to develop a scenario for the ballet.

Poster for Ballets Russes by Cocteau

The choreography for *Le Spectre de la Rose* was created by Fokine in St. Petersburg in a matter of days; it was based entirely on the physical capacities of his dancers, and in Paris the name of this ballet very soon became inseparable from the names of Karsavina and Nijinsky.

Nijinsky's prodigious elevation in this work led the critics to say that he seemed to be painted permanently on the ceiling, and Grigoriev tells us that the night of the Paris première, at the Théâtre du Châtelet on June 6, 1911, "So loud was the applause after Nijinsky's leap from the window that the orchestra was unable to finish playing the music." Diaghilev saw women in the audience faint at Nijinsky's final leap.

However, one evening Nijinsky was indisposed and, at the last moment and without prior announcement, was replaced by Alexander Gavrilov. At the end of the performance, Nijinsky, who was standing in the wings, was surrounded by admirers who had come to tell him that he had never danced better than that evening!

NARCISSE

Classical ballet in one act by Léon Bakst. Music by Nicholas Tcherepnine. Choreography by Michel Fokine. Décor and costumes by Bakst. First performance: Casino, Monte Carlo, April 26, 1911. Principal dancers: Tamara Karsavina, Bronislava Nijinska, Vaslav Nijinsky.

SADKO

"In the kingdom under the sea." Music by Nicholas Rimsky-Korsakov. Choreography by Michel Fokine. Décor and costumes by Boris Anisfeldt. First performance: Théâtre du Châtelet, Paris, June 6, 1911.

Costume design by Léon Bakst

PETROUCHKA

Ballet-burlesque in four scenes by Igor Stravinsky and Alexandre Benois. Music by Stravinsky. Choreography by Michel Fokine. Décor and costumes by Benois. First performance: Théâtre du Châtelet, Paris, June 13, 1911.

In the autumn of 1910, en route to Russia from Venice, Diaghilev stopped off in Switzerland to visit Stravinsky, who played for him his two most recent compositions, a "Russian Dance" and a piece for piano and orchestra entitled "The Cry of Petrouchka."

Diaghilev was overwhelmed; writing to friends from Switzerland, he described the music as works of genius. He persuaded Stravinsky to take these two pieces as a point of departure for a new ballet; thus the piano piece became the second scene in *Petrouchka*, and the "Russian Dance" became the core of the final scene.

Petrouchka, sketch by Alexandre Benois

Stravinsky's original title—"The Cry of Petrouchka"—suggested the role of the ballet's principal character and determined the location of the action, but the definitive version of the plot was worked out by Benois and Stravinsky in the spring of 1911 in Rome.

It was in Rome, also, that Fokine created the ensembles for *Petrouchka*, which he based on folk dances and the day-by-day activities of ordinary Russians. For the dance of the coachmen in the last scene, for example, he took as his model the hack drivers of St. Petersburg, who, in the winter, wait at their stands, clapping their hands, stamping their feet, and thumping each other on the shoulders to keep warm.

The Street Dancer number parodied the conventional style of the premières danseuses of the Imperial Theatre, and caricatured a classical adagio interpreted by Mathilda Kchessinska.

Some of the crowd scenes in *Petrouchka* developed spontaneously and were later adopted by Fokine. During the dress rehearsal, in Paris, one of the walk-ons in the first scene forgot that when the Charlatan came onstage she should move off toward the wings; instead, she stood before him, alone in the middle of the stage, as if she were mesmerized by his flute solo. Fokine was enchanted with this unplanned bit of stage business and kept it in the ballet.

Diaghilev told me later that the conception of the final moments of the production had been dramatic. The evening of the dress rehearsal, Fokine, Benois, and Stravinsky were pacing up and down the Châtelet stage, asking each other what kind of an ending they should devise. It was only a few moments before the curtain went up that Fokine got the idea for the final pantomime, which at the time was an unusual finale for a ballet.

That same evening, an incident occurred that precipitated an extended quarrel between Benois and Bakst. Benois had painted a portrait of the Charlatan on one of the flats for the second scene, and just before the dress rehearsal this had been damaged. Benois was ill, so he asked Bakst to retouch it. When he came to the theatre to check on the retouching, Benois discovered that Bakst had painted out his figure entirely and replaced it with the portrait of a character of his own invention. Benois was outraged; in his fury, he broke with Bakst, broke with Diaghilev and with several other friends who defended Bakst, and resigned from his post as artistic director of the Ballets Russes.

Cecchetti in *Petrouchka*

Because, in 1914, Massine made his debut with the Diaghilev company in the supporting role of the Policeman in *Petrouchka*, to Diaghilev's superstitious mind it became a matter of prime importance that new recruits to the company appear in this ballet. He was convinced that this secondary role brought luck to a dancer who was making his debut, that it guaranteed a brilliant future. When Anton Dolin and, later, Serge Lifar joined the Diaghilev company, he immediately cast them as extras in *Petrouchka*.

The Paris première of *Petrouchka* was a triumph, and the work continued to be one of the great successes of the Ballets Russes until Diaghilev's last season, in 1929. Nonetheless, at its first performance, several prominent musicians criticized Stravinsky's revolutionary music harshly. In his *Souvenirs et Commentaires*, Stravinsky recalls that Rimsky-Korsakov described the *Petrouchka* score in a newspaper article as "Russian vodka mixed with French perfume." Diaghilev repeated to me Ravel's comment—that Stravinsky's music was caviar but that he found a meal consisting exclusively of caviar indigestible.

It was during a lighting rehearsal for *Petrouchka* that Diaghilev began teaching me how to handle the lights for a stage performance. The lesson took place in March, 1921, at the Teatro Real, in Madrid, on my first day with the Ballets Russes company. Until then, I had never been in a theatre except during a performance, and I looked forward to this rehearsal as I would to a new production. But when I came into the theatre by the stage door, I found myself in a building plunged in total darkness. Diaghilev took me by the hand and guided me through a labyrinth of stairways and corridors, which, after the blinding sunshine of the street, seemed to me so many subterranean tunnels. The auditorium was empty. A feeble bulb cast a dim light on the first rows of orchestra seats, which were covered with dust sheets.

Schollar in *Petrouchka*

The curtain rose slowly to reveal an immense stage strewn with chests and baskets; bits of scenery and props were piled in front of unassembled flats; worn backdrops stained by dampness hung forlornly from the flies. In the midst of all this debris, some stage hands in espadrilles were leisurely reassembling a wooden fair booth. A walk-on perched on the prompter's box was struggling to slip into an old bearskin.

What, I asked Diaghilev, were these shambles? "*Petrouchka*," he answered.

Without another word, Diaghilev took a seat in the middle of the orchestra and clapped his hands to signal that he was present. Instantly, the workmen redoubled their pace, the stage was cleared and flooded with light, and Diaghilev began the rehearsal. He gave his instructions in Italian, the only language he was familiar with besides Russian and French, and, in order for the Spaniards to understand him, he kept adding an "*as*" or an "*os*" to each word.

As Diaghilev went on with his work, I saw some weary-faced people, dressed in traveling clothes and carrying valises, cross the stage. Before they disappeared into the wings, they came down to the footlights and respectfully greeted the black pit out front, saying "*Bonjour, Serge Pavlovich!*"

Diaghilev named them for me, one by one: Lydia Sokolova, Lubov Tchernicheva, Stanislas Idzikowski, Tadeo Slavinsky. . . . Not one of these worn and disheveled travelers who had just got off the train bore any resemblance to the supernatural beings I had seen the night before in Paris, whose mere presence had seemed to illuminate the stage of the Ballets Russes.

Diaghilev went patiently ahead with his rehearsal. He showed the electricians how to graduate the intensity of the footlights and stage lights, how to focus the spotlights on the flats so that wrinkles would disappear, faded colors would brighten, and shadows would erase damp or worn areas. Within an hour, he caused a sunny St. Petersburg square to rise on the stage. Then Diaghilev ordered the stage darkened and only the Bengal lights cast reflections on the walls, and when we left the theatre, snow was falling over the deserted city streets. The man costumed as a bear was snoring in the wings.

Spessivtzeva and Lifar in *Swan Lake*

SWAN LAKE

Pantomime ballet in two acts and three scenes by Modest Tchaikovsky. Libretto by Vladimir P. Begitchev and Vasily Geltzer. Music by Peter Ilyich Tchaikovsky. Choreography by Marius Petipa. Décor and costumes by Alexander Golovine and Constantine Korovine. First performance by the Ballets Russes: Covent Garden Theatre, London, November 30, 1911. In this version, choreography for the "Waltz" and "Dance of the Princes" in the second scene by Michel Fokine.

Swan Lake was first presented at the Imperial Theatre of Moscow on February 20, 1877, with choreography by Julius Reisinger. The ballet did not meet with favor—Tchaikovsky attributed the failure to his music—and after several performances it was withdrawn from the repertoire.

On February 17, 1894, *Swan Lake* was first performed at the Maryinsky Theatre, in St. Petersburg, this time in a choreographic version by Petipa and his close collaborator, Lev Ivanov, who since 1885 had been second ballet master of the Maryinsky.

The Diaghilev program notes do not mention Ivanov's name, yet it was the Maryinsky version that was adapted by the Ballets Russes, revised and completed first by Fokine, and later by Bronislava Nijinska and by George Balanchine.

The original *Swan Lake* was in four scenes, but the version Diaghilev presented in London in 1911 was in two acts and three scenes, and when the ballet was revived in 1924, it was reduced to a single act including only the first and third scenes.

At the Covent Garden première, the principal roles were danced by Mathilda Kchessinska and Nijinsky; during Diaghilev's last London season, in 1929, at the same theatre, they were danced by Olga Spessivtzeva and Serge Lifar.

One performance of *Swan Lake* that I shall never forget took place in Turin, in 1927. The orchestra director, Désiré-Émile Inghelbrecht, had been engaged for the tour at the last moment, and he had had no time to rehearse with the company. On opening night, he conducted Spessivtzeva's variation at such a slow tempo that it was very nearly impossible for her to dance. Absorbed in the score, Inghelbrecht was not watching the dancer nor did he hear the corps de ballet tapping their feet to signal the proper tempo to him.

We watched as several times in the course of the variation Spessivtzeva extended one leg in a great développé and remained motionless on point, waiting seconds on end—they seemed interminable—for the measure that would allow her to change position. Upright and unfaltering, she held herself on the point of one foot as if she were being sustained by a partner, and smiled at the marveling audience.

At the end of her variation, the dancers crowding together in the wings gave Spessivtzeva an ovation; they were so furious at Inghelbrecht's incompetence that the moment the performance was over they demanded that Diaghilev dismiss him forthwith. No stationery was at hand in the theatre at midnight, and their petition was written out on a roll of toilet paper.

LE
DIEU BLEU

Ballet in one act by Jean Cocteau and Federigo de Madrazo. Music by Reynaldo Hahn. Choreography by Michel Fokine. Décor and costumes by Léon Bakst. First performance: Théâtre du Châtelet, Paris, May 13, 1912.

After extolling the Ballets Russes in the program notes for the 1911 season, Cocteau designed two posters for the company's production of *Le Spectre de la Rose* in 1912, utilizing portraits of Karsavina and Nijinsky. He also wrote the scenario for one of that season's new ballets, *Le Dieu Bleu*.

The influence of the orientalism of Diaghilev's early ballets on fashion and scenic design affected Cocteau and Hahn, who based their ballet on a Hindu legend. The choreography by Fokine was inspired by bas-reliefs of Brahman temples and by Siamese dances he had seen when a troupe of Siamese dancers had performed in St. Petersburg.

Le Dieu Bleu was not successful and the following year was withdrawn from the Ballets Russes repertoire.

Costume design by Bakst

Nijinsky (left)
and Karsavina
in *Le Dieu Bleu*

———

Nijinsky
and Diaghilev, sketch
by Cocteau

THAMAR

Dance drama in one scene, after a poem by Mikhail Lermontov. Music by Mily Balakirev. Choreography by Michel Fokine. Décor and costumes by Léon Bakst. First performance: Théâtre du Châtelet, Paris, May 20, 1912. Principal dancers: Tamara Karsavina, Adolph Bolm.

L'APRES-MIDI
D'UN
FAUNE

Ballet by Vaslav Nijinsky. Music by Claude Debussy. Choreography by Nijinsky. Décor by Léon Bakst. First performance: Théâtre du Châtelet, Paris, May 29, 1912.

L'*Après-Midi d'un Faune should be danced in the midst of a landscape with trees of zinc.—Stéphane Mallarmé, in the program notes for the May–June, 1912, season of the Ballets Russes in Paris.*

Historians of the Ballets Russes have never been able to establish whether it was Diaghilev, Bakst, or Nijinsky who first had the idea of a ballet based on Debussy's Prelude. Possibly, as in the case of several other Ballets Russes creations, the concept of a theatrical version of this work arose in the course of a conversation, in an exchange of ideas between Diaghilev and members of his entourage who have remained unidentified.

It is certain, however, that it was Diaghilev who obtained Debussy's consent to adapt the Prelude to the stage, although when first approached Debussy had been reserved. When Diaghilev mentioned the possibility of basing a ballet on the music, Debussy asked, "Why?"

L'Après-Midi d'un Faune was Nijinsky's first choreographic effort, and it provoked the first "Ballets Russes scandal." What caused the "scandal" was the revolutionary novelty of the choreography, which was influenced by the rhythmic dances of Jacques Dalcroze, which Diaghilev and Nijinsky had seen early in 1912, at Hellerau.

The Paris public was confused and disappointed by Nijinsky's choreography. In large part, it was "static"; the dancers, barefoot, assumed the stances of figures on classical bas-reliefs and moved rhythmically across the stage, their bodies facing the audience, their heads turned in profile. The airborne Nijinsky was as earthbound as all the other dancers and at no point exhibited the technical virtuosity or the extraordinary elevation that had won him the name of "the new Vestris" and called forth ovations whenever he appeared.

Above all, the public was shocked by the final moments of the ballet, when the Faun expresses his passion for the Nymph who has fled by manipulating her veil in a series of movements that were considered indecent.

At the end of the first performance, Diaghilev detected some shouts of approval amid the general hubbub and ordered the curtain to be rung up and the ballet repeated *in toto*.

L'Après-Midi d'un Faune unleashed a violent controversy in the Paris press. Scandalized attacks by the journalists were countered by eulogies from Odilon Redon and Rodin. In quite another area, this ballet also precipitated a basic reorganization of the company's structure; Nijinsky's being identified as choreographer on the posters was one of the reasons for the departure of Fokine, who until then had been choreographic director of the Ballets Russes.

Nijinsky as the Faun
and Nijinska as the Nymph in
L'Après-Midi d'un Faune

In 1922, when Bronislava Nijinska rejoined the company, Diaghilev decided to restage *L'Après-Midi d'un Faune* and to entrust her with the principal role in the ballet, which her brother had created. For this revival, Diaghilev asked Picasso to prepare a new décor. Picasso accepted the commission but was late in delivering his sketch.

Under pressure from the publisher of the program notes, M. de Brunhoff, Diaghilev, before seeing Picasso's sketch, gave instructions that the announcement of his Paris season, at the Théâtre Mogador, should include the credit line: "New Décor by Picasso." When he received Picasso's sketch, it showed a simple backdrop of a washed-out gray, so Diaghilev hastily withdrew any mention of the artist's name from the program and the author of the décor remained anonymous.

In later years, Nijinsky's choreography was completely distorted by numerous dancers who dispensed with the girls of the corps de ballet and converted the ballet into a male solo.

DAPHNIS ET CHLOE

Choreographic symphony in one act and three scenes by Michel Fokine. Music by Maurice Ravel. Choreography by Fokine. Décor and costumes by Léon Bakst. First performance: Théâtre du Châtelet, Paris, June 8, 1912.

Fired with enthusiasm by the performances of the Ballets Russes during their first Paris season, in 1909 Maurice Ravel accepted a commission from Diaghilev to write *Daphnis et Chloë*.

Bolm in *Daphnis et Chloë*

Ravel was slow in delivering the score, however, and, hoping to speed the work along, in 1911 Diaghilev invited him to St. Petersburg in order to put him in direct touch with Fokine and Bakst. Conversations among the three men so stimulated their imaginations that their talk served only to extend the length of the ballet, and Ravel did not finish *Daphnis et Chloë* until 1912.

The idea of adapting the Longus pastoral tale for the stage was Fokine's; under the influence of Isadora Duncan, he had become passionately interested in the art of ancient Greece. However, Ravel's delay in delivering the score prevented Fokine's choreographing the ballet in 1911, and he substituted *Narcisse*.

The next year, when Fokine finally began *Daphnis et Chloë* rehearsals, Diaghilev's attention was concentrated entirely on Nijinsky's progress with his first choreographic effort, *L'Après-Midi*.

Diaghilev's lack of interest in *Daphnis et Chloë* was the chief reason for Fokine's leaving the Ballets Russes company in June, 1912.

Subsequently, Diaghilev commissioned Ravel to write *La Valse*, the score of which was begun in 1919 and completed in 1920. Diaghilev's plan called for Massine to do the choreography, and he envisaged a set that would reproduce with mirror-like fidelity the auditorium of the Paris Opéra, where he expected to present the ballet.

At the last moment, however, Diaghilev and Ravel disagreed over the scenic concept for *La Valse*, and this contretemps coincided with Massine's departure, all of which led Diaghilev to abandon the ballet's production.

Ravel was stunned by Diaghilev's attitude. Years later, when the opera *L'Enfant et les Sortilèges* was being given its première in Monte Carlo, the two men met in the lounge of the Hôtel de Paris, but Ravel refused to shake hands with Diaghilev.

84

Schollar,
Nijinsky, and
Karsavina in *Jeux*

———

Bakst drawing of
Nijinsky rehearsing *Jeux*

———

Nijinsky in *Jeux*

JEUX

Choreographic scenes by Vaslav Nijinsky. Music by Claude Debussy. Choreography by Nijinsky. Décor and costumes by Léon Bakst. First performance: Théâtre des Champs-Élysées, Paris, May 15, 1913.

After the violent response—enthusiastic or hostile—from both public and press to the presentation of *L'Après-Midi d'un Faune* the year before, *Jeux*, another ballet by the same trio of creators—Debussy, Nijinsky, and Bakst —went almost unnoticed. The more so because *Le Sacre du Printemps*, Nijinsky's major work, was given its first performance two weeks later and became the outstanding event of this Diaghilev season, casting the other new ballets into the shade.

Nonetheless, in certain details the choreography for *Jeux* seems to have been a preliminary study for Nijinsky in developing *Le Sacre*. For example, photographs of the three dancers in *Jeux* show them in "anticlassical" poses—arms rounded, fingers pressed together, feet turned inward. But these unusual positions alternated with purely classical dance steps and, according to Diaghilev, the high point of *Jeux* was its opening, when Nijinsky, with a grand jeté, appeared onstage in pursuit of a tennis ball.

LE
SACRE DU
PRINTEMPS

Ballet of pagan Russia in two scenes by Igor Stravinsky and Nicholas Roerich. Music by Stravinsky. Choreography by Vaslav Nijinsky. Mise-en-scène by Stravinsky and Nijinsky. Décor and costumes by Roerich. First performance: Théâtre des Champs-Élysées, Paris, May 29, 1913. First performance of the new version, with choreography by Leonide Massine: Théâtre des Champs-Élysées, Paris, December 15, 1920.

The première of *Le Sacre du Printemps* was a historic date in the development of contemporary music and dance. The boldness of Stravinsky's score and of Nijinsky's choreography, which conflicted with the century-old code of the classical ballet, raised a great outcry among the public and the press. Few persons who attended the opening of *Le Sacre* doubted that this revolutionary work was ushering in a new era in the history of music and dance.

Ensemble, 1920 version by Massine

In *Le Coq et l'Arlequin*, Jean Cocteau describes the audience's reactions at the first performance:

. . . Let us go back into the theatre on Avenue Montaigne and wait for the orchestra leader to tap his music stand and for the curtain to rise on one of the most noble events in the annals of art.

The audience played the role that it had to play: it instantly rebelled. People talked, booed, whistled, imitated animal cries. Perhaps they would have grown tired eventually if a group of aesthetes and some musicians had not been carried away by an excess of zeal and insulted, even jostled, the audience in the loges. The uproar degenerated into a pitched battle.

Standing in her box, her diadem askew, the elderly Comtesse de Pourtalès brandished her fan and, in a positive frenzy, cried, "This is the first time in sixty years that anyone has dared make fun of me!" The good lady was sincere; she really believed it was all a practical joke.

And so we were introduced to this historic work in the midst of such a tumult that the dancers could no longer hear the orchestra and had to take the beat from Nijinsky, who was prancing and yelling in the wings.

Nijinsky's work (in which he was assisted by Marie Rambert, then a student at the Dalcroze School of Eurhythmics), his search for new plastic movement, and the retraining of dancers who from the outset of their studies had obeyed the academic rules which Nijinsky was fighting in *Le Sacre*, required a hundred and twenty rehearsals. For months, dancers who had schooled themselves to give the public the impression of weightlessness had to learn to "weight" their bodies; instead of rising on point, they had to learn to turn around on their heels, their feet toed inward.

Nijinsky's *Le Sacre du Printemps* was performed six times in all during the 1913 season, in Paris and in London.

In 1920, Leonide Massine created a new version of the ballet, based in large part on the principles Nijinsky had worked out.

At that time, Diaghilev once again found himself in serious financial difficulties, and was seeking a subsidy or loan so that he could restage *Le Sacre*. Because the Stravinsky score demanded a large orchestra and because orchestra and dancers required an abnormal number of rehearsals, the cost of the undertaking was exorbitant, and it was only thanks to a stroke of luck that Diaghilev was able to go ahead.

During his summer vacation in Venice in 1920, Diaghilev saw Misia Sert every day, and often Mme. Sert was accompanied by a young woman friend whom Diaghilev had not known before and whose name he did not remember. The young woman would sit and listen in silence as Diaghilev talked with Mme. Sert and bemoaned the lack of funds for new productions.

Back in Paris and still unable to find financial backing, Diaghilev was growing more and more discouraged when one morning, at the hotel where he was living, he was informed that a Mlle. C—— was calling. Diaghilev did not recognize the name but, nevertheless, he reluctantly agreed to receive the unknown caller.

When he arrived downstairs in the lobby, Diaghilev found himself face to face with the friend of Mme. Sert, who said to him, "I heard your conversations with Misia in Venice, and I know about your difficulties. I've come to help you—on the condition that you never speak of it to anyone." And she handed Diaghilev a check exceeding his wildest hopes.

Talking to me about the visit of Mlle. C——, who later became one of his closest friends, Diaghilev broke his promise of silence, which is how I can repeat the story and name the lady—Gabrielle Chanel.

First offered in its restaged form at the Théâtre des Champs-Élysées on December 15, 1920, *Le Sacre* was a triumphal success. Presented in London a few months later, the ballet had to be withdrawn from the repertoire after two performances.

At the second performance, the Princess Theatre was empty. The English public was conservative, it cherished memories of Diaghilev's early productions, and had been put off by the London reviews; it would come to see only those performances in which this ballet was not included.

During the 1924 Ballets Russes season in Paris, at the Théâtre des Champs-Élysées, Diaghilev presented on June 13 a comic opera by Emmanuel Chabrier, *L'Éducation Manquée*, for which Juan Gris designed the sets and Darius Milhaud wrote the recitatifs.

Diaghilev's repertoire for his Paris opera season was limited to productions he had already presented that January in Monte Carlo. In addition to the Chabrier work, there were three operas by Gounod: *Le Médecin Malgré Lui*, *Philémon et Baucis*, and *La Colombe*, for which Diaghilev had Erik Satie and Francis Poulenc compose additional recitatifs.

At the opening performance of *L'Éducation Manquée* in Paris, the orchestra was conducted by André Messager, and the cast included Inès Ferraris, Geneviève Vix, and Daniel Vigneau.

From the start, it was a stormy première. The habitual audience for Diaghilev productions was disappointed to find that an opera had replaced a ballet; also, people were thrown off by the music, which they found boring and banal, and they gave vent to their feelings noisily indeed. Thereafter, Chabrier's opera was replaced by *Le Sacre du Printemps*, which, as Diaghilev put it, had become a "perfectly safe" ballet.

SALOME

Ballet after a poem by Robert d'Humières. Music by Florent Schmitt. Choreography by Boris Romanov. Curtain, décor, and costumes by Serge Soudeikine. First performance: Théâtre des Champs-Élysées, Paris, June 12, 1913.

When Fokine left the company in June, 1912, Diaghilev was anxious to spare Nijinsky the burden of creating all the works for the next Ballets Russes season. His intention was to entrust the choreography for a new ballet by Tcherepnine, *Les Masques Rouges*, to Alexander Gorsky, ballet master of the Imperial Theatre of Moscow, and the choreography for *Salomé* to Boris Romanov.

The plan to engage Gorsky came to nothing and Tcherepnine's ballet was never produced. However, Romanov, who had been a student of Fokine and was the leading character dancer at the Maryinsky Theatre in St. Petersburg, arrived from Russia to choreograph Florent Schmitt's ballet.

This was Romanov's first choreographic venture, as it was the theatrical debut of the young Russian painter Serge Soudeikine.

Despite the importance of Schmitt's score and the participation of Tamara Karsavina (before every performance, Soudeikine himself undertook to paint a rose on her knee), *Salomé* met with no success and was performed only in Paris and London in 1913.

However, in 1914 Diaghilev re-engaged Romanov to create the dances for Stravinsky's opera *Le Rossignol*, which was first performed on May 26, during the Ballets Russes season at the Paris Opéra.

LES PAPILLONS

Ballet in one act by Michel Fokine. (Sequel to *Le Carnaval*.) Music by Robert Schumann, orchestrated by Nicholas Tcherepnine. Choreography by Michel Fokine. Décor by Mstislav Doboujinsky. Costumes by Léon Bakst. First performance: Casino, Monte Carlo, April 16, 1914.

When Michel Fokine returned to the Ballets Russes, he remembered the success of *Carnaval* and had the idea of creating another ballet to a score by the same composer, Schumann.

In designing the women's costumes for both *Carnaval* and *Papillons*, Bakst drew on the Biedermeier style; he worked from German fashion engravings of the 1830's, and for the principal male dancer in *Papillons* he designed, as he had for *Carnaval*, a Pierrot costume.

Karsavina danced the leading female role in both ballets, but the absence of Nijinsky, who had enjoyed a triumph in *Carnaval*, was deeply felt in *Papillons*.

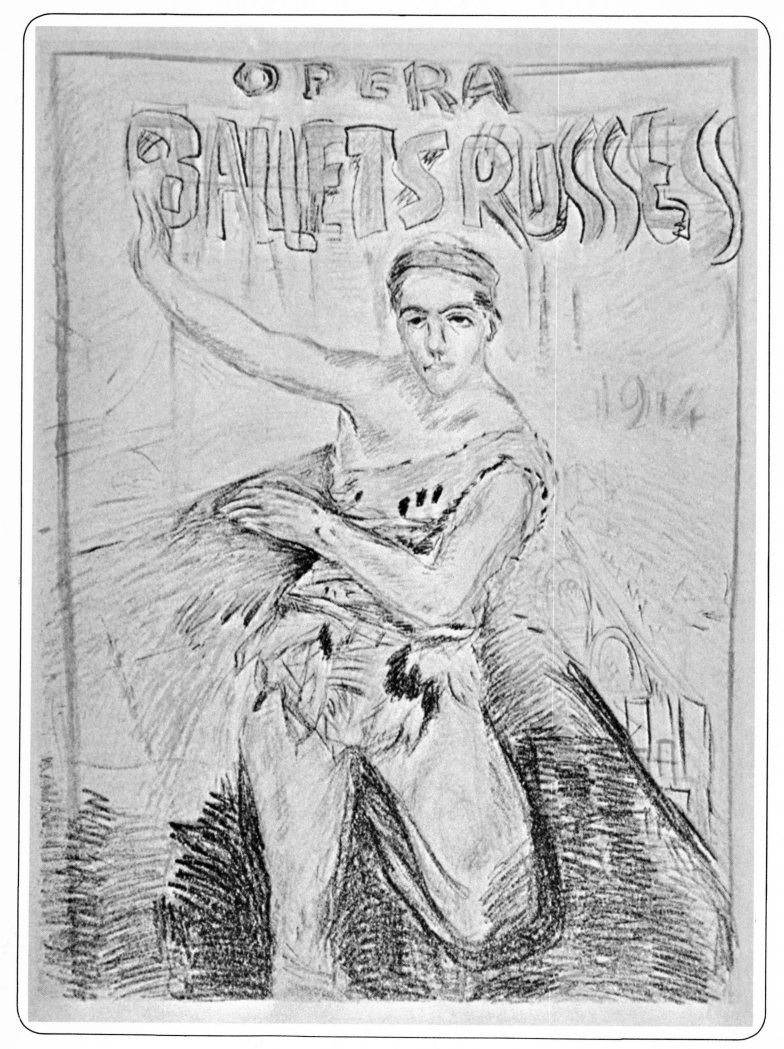

Massine in *The Legend of Joseph*; sketch for poster by Pierre Bonnard

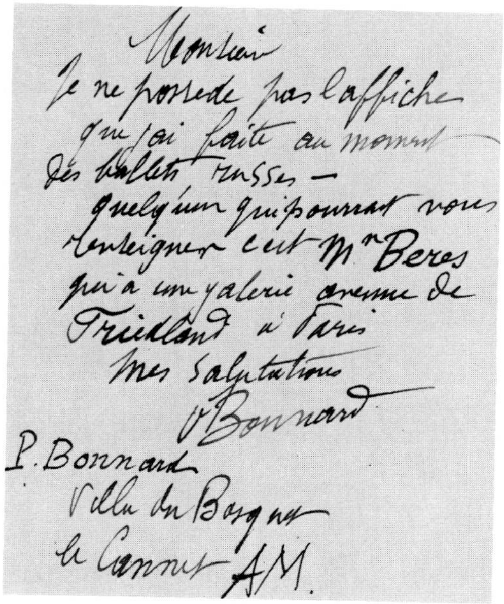

Monsieur
Je ne possède pas l'affiche
que j'ai faite au moment
des ballets russes —
quelqu'un qui pourrait vous
renseigner c'est M*r* Berès
qui a une galerie avenue de
Friedland à Paris
Mes salutations
P. Bonnard

P. Bonnard
Villa du Bosquet
le Cannet A.M.

THE
LEGEND OF JOSEPH

Ballet in one act. Libretto by Count Harry Kessler and Hugo von Hofmannsthal. Music by Richard Strauss. Choreography by Michel Fokine. Décor by José-Maria Sert. Costumes by Léon Bakst. First performance: Théâtre National de l'Opéra, Paris, May 17, 1914. (In Grigoriev's chronological list of the Diaghilev ballets, he gives the date of the ballet's Paris première as May 17, 1914, while Massine assigns it the date of May 14 of the same year.)

In December, 1913, Diaghilev saw Leonide Massine dance the Tarantella in *Swan Lake* at the Imperial Theatre of Moscow, where Massine had made his debut in 1912 upon leaving the Imperial Ballet School. He engaged Massine for the leading role in *La Légende de Joseph*.

Diaghilev had intended to entrust both the leading role and the choreography to Nijinsky, but after their break as a result of Nijinsky's sudden marriage and his leaving the company, Diaghilev asked Fokine to create the new ballet.

Later, in connection with the unforeseen departure of several other of the company's premiers danseurs, I heard Diaghilev say, "No one is irreplaceable."

Diaghilev commissioned Richard Strauss to compose the score for *La Légende*, in anticipation of the Ballets Russes's important Berlin season in October, 1914, but the First World War prevented his giving any performances in Germany, and the ballet was produced only in Paris and London.

Despite the importance of the Strauss score (the composer conducted at the première) and the sumptuous mise-en-scène by Sert and Bakst, which was inspired by Venetian painting of the Renaissance, particularly the work of Tintoretto and Veronese, *La Légende de Joseph* was not the theatrical event that Diaghilev had expected.

In the mimed role of Potiphar's wife, the singer Maria Kuznetsova disappointed the public. As for Massine, his success was due to his physique, the Byzantine beauty of his face, and the suppleness of his youthful body. (Born in 1895, Massine was then barely nineteen.)

Diaghilev had not liked Bakst's sketch for Massine's costume, and he ordered a new sketch from Benois. This costume was a simple goatskin tunic, which led Parisians to dub the ballet "*Les Jambes de Joseph*."

LE COQ D'OR

Opera in three acts, by Nicholas Rimsky-Korsakov. Mise-en-scène and choreography by Michel Fokine. Décor and costumes by Nathalie Gontcharova. First performance: Théâtre National de l'Opéra, Paris, May 21, 1914.

In his book, *The Diaghilev Ballet: 1909–1929*, Serge Grigoriev writes:

Diaghilev and his friends would often bemoan the inability of opera singers, with the exception of a few such as Chaliapine, to act; and Benois had more than once remarked how pleasant it would be if the singers could remain hidden and their parts mimed for them by a cast of actors. Now, therefore, in our predicament over the subject for a new ballet, he suggested quite seriously our trying this with another opera of Rimsky-Korsakov's, Le Coq d'Or, letting the characters be presented on the stage by dancers, while the singers were concealed in the orchestra pit. Diaghilev was immediately fired with this idea, and declared that it must be tried. To begin with, it was proposed that only a few scenes should be so treated, but in the end it was decided to perform the whole work in this way. Fokine was also much taken with the suggestion and began at once inventing action to illustrate the story in conformity with the music.

Despite the ballet's triumphal success in Paris and London, Rimsky-Korsakov's widow disapproved of the choreographed version of the opera and forbade Diaghilev to present it again.

MIDAS

Mythological comedy in one act by Léon Bakst after Ovid's *Metamorphoses*. Music by Maximilian Steinberg. Choreography by Michel Fokine. Décor and costumes by Mstislav Doboujinsky. (In the program for *Midas*, décor and costumes were credited to Bakst.) First performance: Théâtre National de l'Opéra, Paris, June 2, 1914.

Midas was the last ballet Fokine created for the Diaghilev company. The score was written by a Russian composer, Maximilian Steinberg, born in Vilna in 1883. Steinberg had been a pupil of Rimsky-Korsakov (whose son-in-law he was also) and of Glazounov at the St. Petersburg Conservatory. The décor and costumes by Doboujinsky were inspired by Mantegna's "Il Parnasso."

After a very few performances in Paris and London in 1914, *Midas* was withdrawn from the repertoire of the Ballets Russes.

Bolm in *Midas*

LITURGIE

Diaghilev had undertaken the cultural education of Massine as soon as his choreographer-to-be arrived in Europe, and during their long trip to Italy in the fall of 1914 this became his principal concern. Their days were devoted largely to visiting museums, old churches, and exhibitions of the young Futurist painters.

In the course of introducing Massine to early Italian painting in Florence and Rome, and to the Byzantine mosaics in Ravenna, Diaghilev conceived the project of a ballet based on religious themes—a kind of Eastern Orthodox mystery-ballet. He gave it the working title of *Liturgie* and planned to commission Stravinsky to write the score. A scholar in liturgical music, Mestrovič, was to assist Stravinsky.

On November 25, 1914, Diaghilev wrote to Stravinsky from Rome:

> . . . *what I have in mind is a stage performance of the Mass in six or seven short scenes; period, High Byzantine. The music would be a series of a cappella religious choruses, modeled perhaps on the Gregorian chant, but more likely on a later style. When you come [to Rome], you will meet a great connoisseur of early Church music: Mestrovič.*

(Left) Stravinsky and Massine, 1915

Costume design by Nathalie Gontcharova for *Liturgie*

Further on in the same letter, Diaghilev wrote: "I am working with him [Mestrovič] and Massine. Heaven protect us! I want to entrust Massine with the choreography of this ballet."

After a meeting in Rome with Diaghilev and Mestrovič, Stravinsky, who disapproved of the idea of presenting the Mass on the stage, refused to write the score, and in 1915, in Switzerland, Massine began to devise the choreography for *Liturgie* without benefit of any music.

Disappointed in the results of this venture, Diaghilev wrote to Stravinsky from Rome, on March 8, 1915:

> *After twenty-two rehearsals of* Liturgie, *we have come to the conclusion that absolute silence is death. . . . Therefore, the dance action will have to be supported not by music but by sounds—that is to say, by filling the ear with harmonies.*

Diaghilev explored such a sound accompaniment with Filippo Marinetti's Futurist orchestra, but although Massine's work was well advanced and many designs for the mise-en-scène had been prepared by Nathalie Gontcharova, the ballet was never completed.

The first scene of *Liturgie* was a staging of the Annunciation. The role of the Virgin Mary was to have been interpreted by Lydia Sokolova, and Massine was to have danced the Archangel Gabriel.

THE
MIDNIGHT SUN

Russian scenes and dances by Leonide Massine. Music by Nicholas Rimsky-Korsakov. Choreography by
Leonide Massine. Décor and costumes by Michel Larionov. First performance: Grand Théâtre, Geneva,
December 20, 1915.

In 1915, after he had abandoned his plan to
produce *Liturgie*, Diaghilev decided that Massine should compose a ballet to the dance
music in Rimsky-Korsakov's *The Snow Maiden*. He entitled it provisionally *Le Soleil de
Minuit*; later, the title was changed to *Le Soleil de Nuit*.

During the *Liturgie* rehearsals, Diaghilev had invited Nathalie Gontcharova and her
husband, Michel Larionov, to Ouchy, outside Lausanne, where Massine was working on the
choreography. Gontcharova was to do designs for the mise-en-scène, and Diaghilev appointed Larionov to supervise Massine's choreography.

Larionov was passionately interested in every form of theatrical expression, particularly
in the dance, and he was, furthermore, a great connoisseur of Russian folklore. He guided
Massine in his work not only for *Liturgie* but also for *Le Soleil de Nuit*; the latter, which
was Massine's first ballet to be publicly performed, was the result of their close collaboration.

Costume design by José-Maria Sert

LAS MENINAS

A Pavane. Music by Gabriel Fauré. Choreography by Leonide Massine. Décor by Carlo Sokrate. Costumes by José-Maria Sert. First performance: Teatro Eugenia-Victoria, San Sebastián, August 21, 1916.

In April, 1919, in the program for the Ballets Russes performances at the Alhambra Theatre, in London, Diaghilev announced the production of a new ballet, *Les Jardins d'Aranjuez. Las Meninas* was to be incorporated in it, but the larger work was never completed.

The Gardens of Aranjuez

Three Old-Time Dances by Leonide Massine. Music by Fauré, Ravel, and Chabrier. Prelude by Louis Aubert. Scenery and costumes by José-Maria Sert.

Synopsis

These three dances belong to the reign of Philip IV, the time of Velásquez. The first of them is a Pavane to music by Gabriel Fauré, danced by ladies and gentlemen of the Court, who seize the opportunity for a little flirtation. They are interrupted by a duenna, whose ungainliness makes her envious of the gracious scene, and who steals the hat of one of the nobles. The second dance, based on Ravel's "Alborada of Gracioso" is, as the title indicates, the morning song of a comic poet, who, followed by four buffoons, pays his court to Donna Sol. The third, in which all take part, is a Menuet Pompeux by Chabrier, specially orchestrated for this occasion by Ravel.

TYL EULENSPIEGEL

Dramatic comedy-ballet by Vaslav Nijinsky. Music by Richard Strauss. Décor and costumes by Robert Edmond Jones. Choreography by Nijinsky. First performance: Manhattan Opera House, New York, October 23, 1916.

At the beginning of the war Nijinsky had been interned in Hungary. After being liberated in 1916, thanks to Diaghilev's intervention, he returned to the company. Wanting to free himself from Diaghilev's influence, he made complete creative independence the condition on which he agreed to return.

At the time of the Ballets Russes's second tour of the United States, which Diaghilev decided not to accompany, Nijinsky took over the direction of the troupe and produced *Tyl Eulenspiegel* in New York. As a result Diaghilev was unaware of the evolution of *Tyl Eulenspiegel* and never saw the ballet, which had several performances in the United States only.

Diaghilev told me that in the period when they worked together Nijinsky had spoken to him of a projected ballet which would begin with a *tableau vivant* in which pregnant women would sit motionless on rows of chairs in front of the bare walls of an immense unfurnished room. The spectacle of the women with bulging stomachs, reminiscent of the side views of women in some paintings of the Middle Ages, might have had a certain connection with Nijinsky's vision of *Tyl Eulenspiegel*, the Flemish legend dating from the same era.

In 1917 Nijinsky took part in the Ballets Russes tours of Spain, Brazil and the Argentine, and his last appearance in a Diaghilev production was in Buenos Aires on September 16, 1917. But the first symptoms of his mental imbalance put in an appearance before he left for South America, and in June, 1917, Diaghilev telegraphed from Barcelona to the directors of the Teatro Colón in Buenos Aires:

NIJINSKY HAS STIRRED UP ENORMOUS DIFFICULTIES POLICE HAD TO ARREST HIM YESTERDAY TO PREVENT HIS RUNNING OFF THEREFORE HIS ARRIVAL IN THE ARGENTINE IMPROBABLE.

After returning to Europe, Nijinsky, ill, established himself in Switzerland, where he tried to go back to performing. The conductor, Ernest Ansermet, a friend of Diaghilev, described in a letter the result of these efforts:

Geneva*Geneva, August 21, 1919*

. . . Some friends I ran into have told me of attending a benefit performance given by Nijinsky two or three months ago at Suvretta-Haus near St. Moritz (Engadine).

The dancer appeared in work clothes covered by a dressing gown. His sister-in-law was at the piano. He announced that he would not perform any precise program but would dance improvisations. Then he ran up and down the stage, attached little ribbons to his legs, collected his thoughts, and after approximately half-an-hour told the pianist to begin playing. He then made certain motions with his head and stopped the pianist saying: "It's too banal." She began with something else. New attempts at mime. New interruptions: "It's too sad." Several attempts to change the ribbons were made, with long pauses in between. And then, abruptly, it was all over. The spectators left in a rage, declaring Nijinsky must be a fake.

Karsavina
and Diaghilev
with Nijinsky
at the Paris Opéra,
1929

I saw Nijinsky for the first time when he visited the Ballets Russes rehearsal at the Théâtre Mogador in Paris, in June, 1922. Diaghilev had learned that Nijinsky was in Paris and decided to make one last attempt to bring him back to his senses, to life and to the dance. His intention was clear: to rouse Nijinsky from his torpor by reminding him of what he loved most, the ballet. And so, one day, we saw Nijinsky, helped by a male nurse, make his way laboriously into the rehearsal room of the theatre. Although the dancers, most of them comrades who had danced beside him, had been alerted the evening before, they rushed to meet him. But confronting his blind stare, calm and absent, they immediately drew back, their eyes full of tears.

Diaghilev signaled the rehearsal to begin. The dancers took their places and we heard the opening measures of *Le Sacre du Printemps*, for which, in 1912, Nijinsky had created the astounding choreography.

At that moment one might have believed in miracles, because suddenly, as he heard Stravinsky's music, his face, impassive until then, began to change expression, his glance came to life, and he puckered his eyebrows; he seemed to be making an effort to remember something, and he started to get up from his chair. Suddenly, as if two invisible hands had fallen on his shoulders, Nijinsky fell back into the chair, and we beheld the same waxen face and dead stare we had seen when he arrived.

THE
GOOD-HUMORED
LADIES

Ballet in one act, after the play *Le Donne di Buon Umore*, by Carlo Goldoni, and adapted by Vincenzo Tommasini. Music by Domenico Scarlatti, orchestrated by Tommasini. Choreography by Leonide Massine. Décor and costumes by Léon Bakst. First performance: Teatro Costanzi, Rome, April 12, 1917.

Massine created his first important ballet, *Les Femmes de Bonne Humeur*, in 1916, in Rome. With this work, he showed himself to be a great choreographer and immediately established his personal style. He had recently discovered dance manuals and choreographers' notes from the seventeenth and eighteenth centuries; they stimulated his development as a creator of dance and served as the basis for the choreography both of *Les Femmes de Bonne Humeur* and of his later ballets.

The idea of a dance version of Goldoni's comedy had been Diaghilev's, and it was he who put together the score for the ballet from Scarlatti's piano sonatas, which he had Tommasini orchestrate.

Massine in
The Good-Humored Ladies

Lopoukhova in
The Good-Humored Ladies

M. and Mme. Cecchetti in
The Good-Humored Ladies

111

Diaghilev commissioned Bakst to design the décor and costumes. Bakst was fearful of losing his reputation as an innovator, which he had won with his first mise-en-scènes for the Ballets Russes, and he was, furthermore, obsessed by the success of the Cubists. The proposal he submitted to Diaghilev for the set represented a Venetian square as if seen in a convex mirror, all the architectural forms being curved. Diaghilev rejected this scheme, and Bakst produced a new design for a realistic décor.

The appearance of the Ballets Russes in Rome included the première of *Les Femmes de Bonne Humeur* and a production of Stravinsky's *Fireworks*, a spectacle consisting of the play of lights, in a setting by the Futurist artist Giacomo Balla.

LES CONTES RUSSES

Three choreographic miniatures, with danced Interludes and an Epilogue. Music by Anatole Liadov. Choreography by Leonide Massine. Décor and costumes by Michel Larionov. First performance: Théâtre du Châtelet, Paris, May 11, 1917.

The first section of *Les Contes Russes*, entitled "Kikimora," was performed for the first time on August 25, 1916, at the Teatro Eugenia-Victoria in San Sebastián.

The following year, in Rome, Massine completed the ballet in collaboration with Larionov, adding two other episodes taken from Russian legends—"Bova Korolevich" and "Baba-Yaga"—and connecting them by folk dances.

This was not yet the definitive version of *Les Contes Russes*, however. For the company's London season in December, 1918, at the Coliseum, Massine reworked the choreography and Larionov proposed adding a pas de deux for Bova and the Swan Princess.

On December 5, 1918, he wrote Diaghilev, mentioning this pas de deux and suggesting some costume changes:

The colors of the Swan Princess's costume (I don't know how this will strike you) should be delicate shades: thus her tights are pale pearl-gray-rose and not the aniline red worn endlessly by dancers. . . . Those parts of the costume which in the drawing are sketched in gray should be silver lamé. . . . Her scarf should be pale blue. . . .

This is how her entrance should be staged: she appears floating above the stage, pursued by Bova, who holds the end of her scarf. Bova bounds onstage as if he too were flying, as though the scarf were holding him up. Then the scarf falls to the ground, and the couple execute their pas de deux. The effect of the dancer's emerging from a sort of spark-filled fog and of Bova's seeming to brush it aside may work out pretty well, if you like the idea. . . . In this scene, the dancer's tights can be pale blue and her slippers pearl-gray rose. Her face also can be pale blue, and her cheeks not rouged but touched with a dark blue.

As for the costume for the Czarevitch [Bova], the areas that I have left in white on the sketch should be worked out in silver lamé. His shield bears a red sun.

Bova might wear a silver mask. This mask must not be of a dull metal, but covered with high-gloss silver leaf. His gloves of the same material. The mask could have the features indicated in my sketch, or it could reproduce Massine's own face, with the eyes, mouth, and nose outlined in niello. This will produce the effect of an icon embellished with risas, although in an actual icon it is just the reverse (but for us better this way).

(In Russia, painted icons were habitually covered with risas—i.e., plaques of silver or enamel—so that only the faces and the hands of the saints were visible.)

Larionov's plans were never carried out, and the version Massine created in 1918 was the definitive form of *Les Contes Russes*.

Set for *Les Contes Russes*, by Michel Larionov

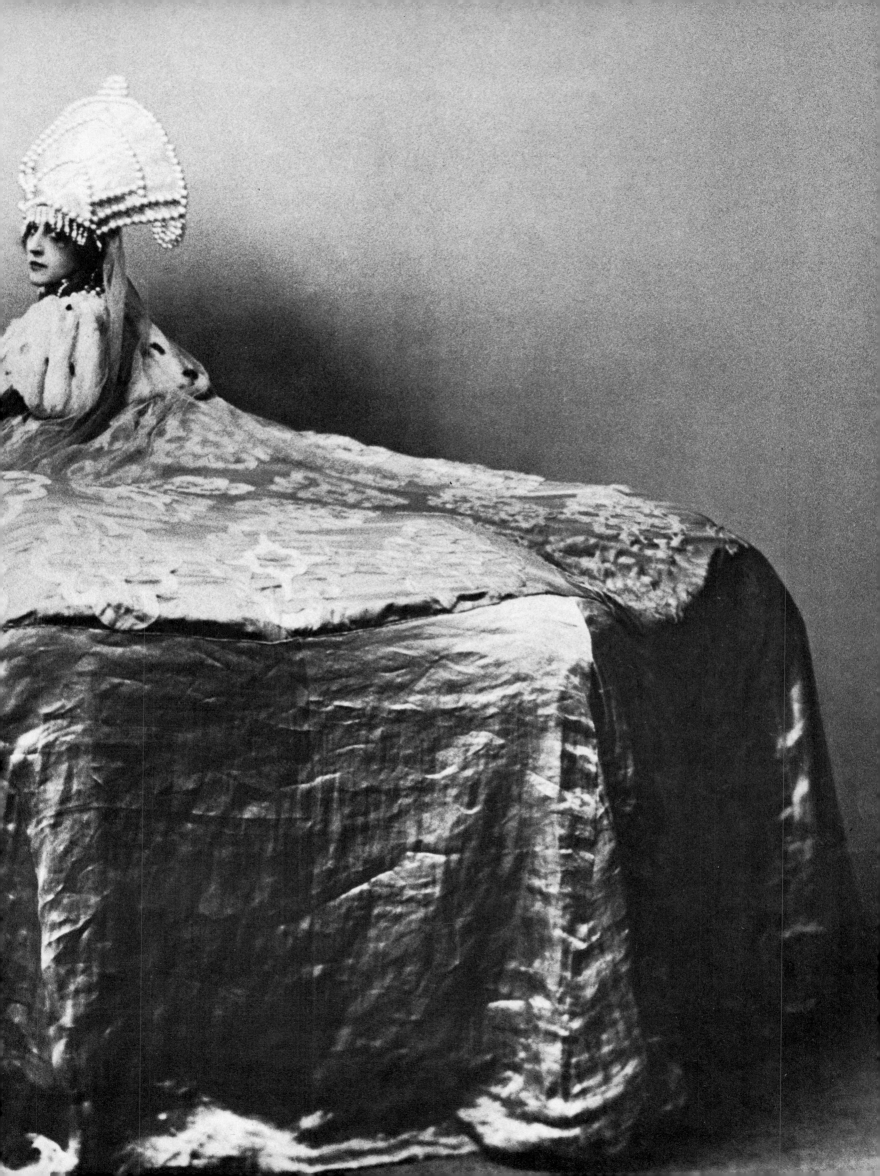

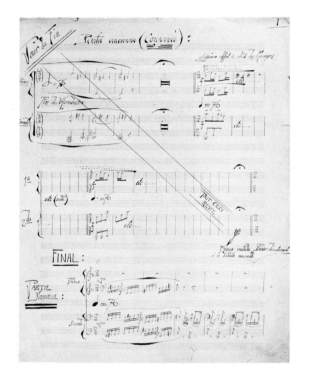

PARADE

Realistic ballet in one scene, on a theme by Jean Cocteau. Music by Erik Satie. Choreography by Leonide Massine. Curtain, décor, and costumes by Pablo Picasso. First performance: Théâtre du Châtelet, Paris, May 18, 1917.

In *Le Coq et l'Arlequin*, Jean Cocteau tells us that the first draft of the libretto for *Parade* was actually a ballet project called *David* that he had sketched out in 1914. The action of this ballet was to take place in front of the entrance to a booth in a traveling fair, and Cocteau describes it thus:

An acrobat would do his pitch for David, *the big show supposedly presented inside; a clown, who would then become a box, the theatrical equivalent of the fair phonograph, the modern version of the ancient mask, would sing through a megaphone of the prowess of David and entreat the public to enter and see the show inside.*

David never got written, however, and Cocteau's first contacts with Satie date from 1915, while his collaboration with Picasso began the following year.

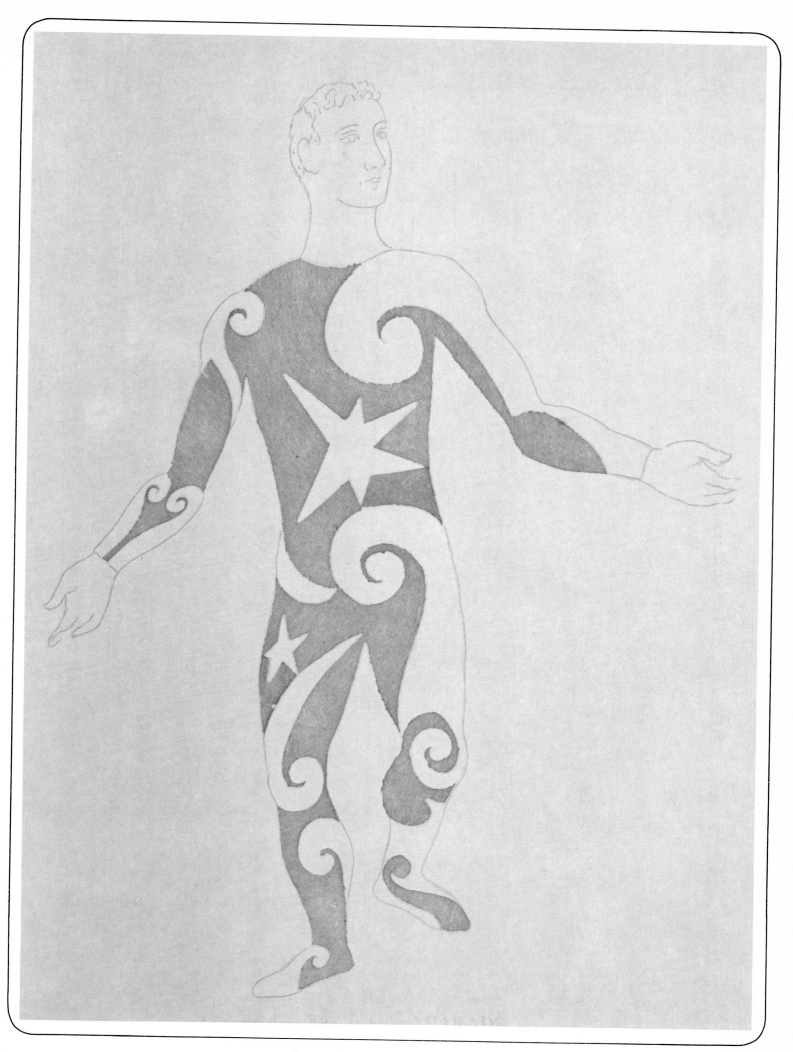

Costume design for *Parade*, by Picasso

A Ansermet
son ami Picasso
à Barcelona
1917

Picasso and
workmen constructing the
set for *Parade*

Diaghilev had met Picasso in the spring of 1916, taken to his studio in Montparnasse by their mutual friend, Mme. Eugenia Errazuriz; it was then that he commissioned Picasso to design the mise-en-scène for *Parade*.

In February, 1917, Picasso and Cocteau went to Rome, where the Diaghilev company was rehearsing, in order to work with Massine, and in March they followed the company to Naples. It was during the company's stay in Rome that Picasso met Olga Koklova, a second-ranking dancer in the troupe, whom he married in 1918 in Paris.

Their mutual understanding and Massine's admiration for Picasso made collaboration easy and friendly. The one point on which the coauthors of *Parade* disagreed had to do with the "sound effects"—the barkers' cries and a medley of other noises—that Cocteau wanted integrated into the Satie score. But thanks to the intervention of Diaghilev, Picasso, and Massine, the spielers' patter was eliminated from the ballet and the noisemaking reduced to a minimum.

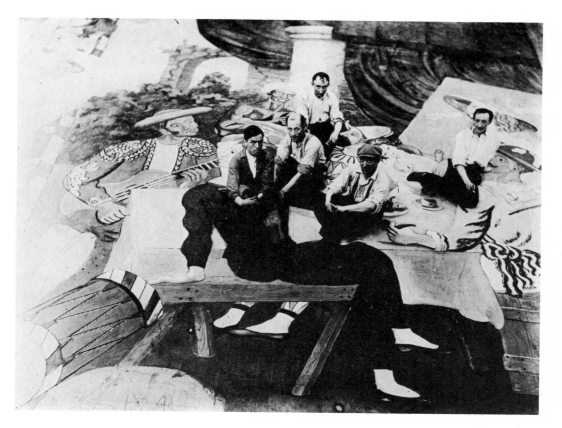

To simplify production problems when *Parade* would be on tour, the orchestral director, Ernest Ansermet, had arranged for Cocteau's "sound machines" to be replaced by musical instruments. A letter that Ansermet wrote in 1917 to Diaghilev in Barcelona allows us to reconstruct the original version of this ballet score:

For Parade *you will manage the jangle in whatever way local facilities allow. In Madrid, I had the woodwinds and brasses take over for the "typewriters," and I replaced the "wheel of fortune" with a rattle; "squishy puddles" were achieved with cymbals and sponge-tipped drumsticks, and the bottle-phone became a combination of celesta and campanelli; organ pipes were replaced by a contra bassoon.*

Subsequently, Diaghilev limited Cocteau's "background sound" for *Parade* to the typewriter noises, yet as late as 1923 Satie was writing him: "I don't much care for Jean's noises. But about that there's nothing to be done. We are dealing with a lovable maniac."

Among the characters in *Parade*, Picasso had designed a horse mounted by a Manager, a Negro mannequin in tails and top hat; at the dress rehearsal, the mannequin rider, which had been poorly made, fell off its horse, which made the audience laugh and made Picasso decide to leave it out.

The costume for the American Girl, for which Picasso had not done a sketch, was bought the day before the première at Williams, the sportswear shop. For the costume of the Female Acrobat, a role that Massine introduced into the ballet at the last moment, Picasso painted some spiral designs directly onto the tights Lydia Lopoukhova was to wear.

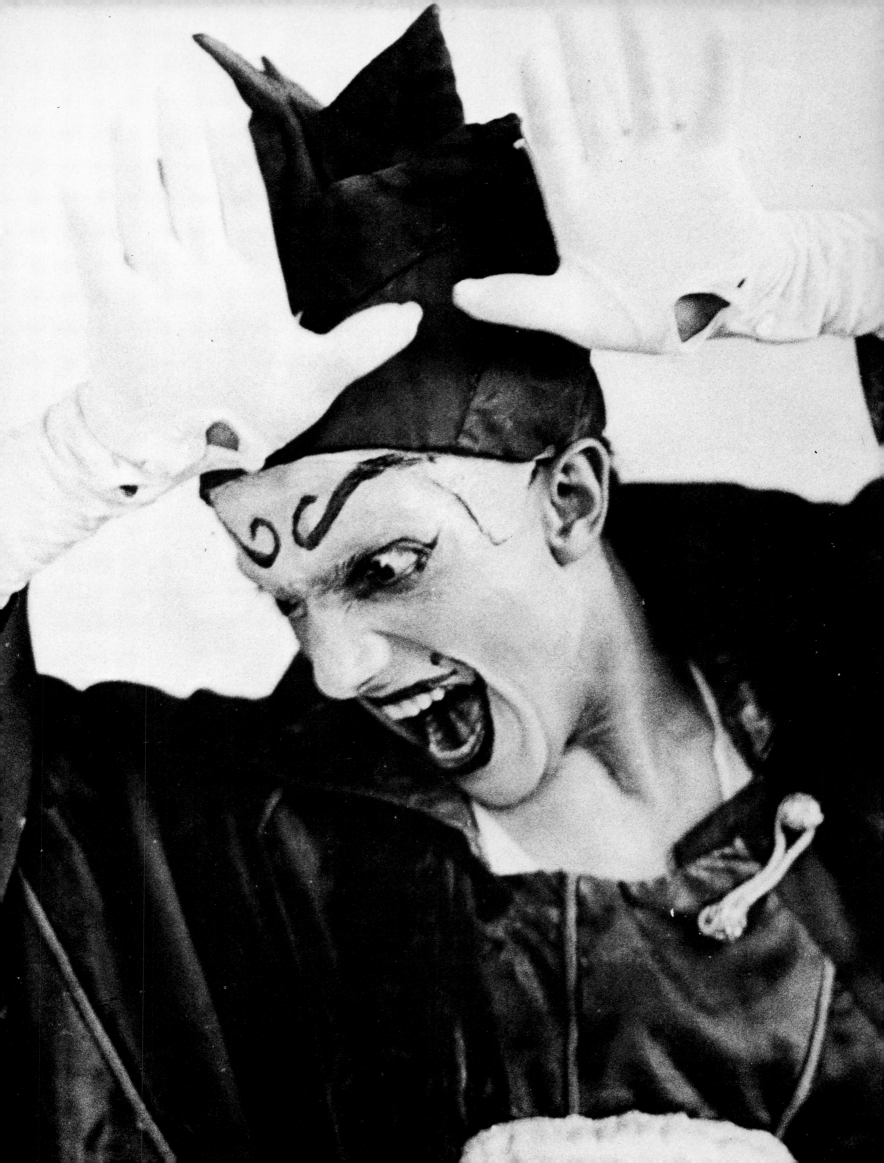

In May, 1917, after an absence of three years, the Ballets Russes returned to Paris and presented *Parade*. It was the pioneer Cubist theatrical spectacle, and in the program notes for its production at the Théâtre du Châtelet, Diaghilev published a piece by Guillaume Apollinaire:

Parade and the New Idea

The definitions of Parade *blossom on all sides, like the lilac branches in this late-blooming spring. . . .*

It is a scenic poem transposed by that innovative musician Erik Satie into astonishingly expressive music, so clear and so simple that in it one will recognize the marvelously lucid mind of France itself.

The Cubist painter Pablo Picasso and that most audacious of choreographers, Leonide Massine, have created it, consummating for the first time an alliance of painting and dance, of the plastic and the mimic, that obviously signals the arrival of a more nearly complete art.

Let no one shout "Paradox!" The Ancients, in whose life music occupied so great a place, knew absolutely nothing of harmony, which is almost the whole of modern music.

Until now, scenery and costumes, on the one hand, and choreography, on the other, have had only an artificial connection, but their fresh alliance in Parade *has produced a kind of Surrealism in which I see the point of departure for further developments of this New Idea, which, having now found the opportunity to manifest itself, will surely seduce the cognoscenti. It promises utterly to transform arts and customs alike in a universal gaiety, for common sense demands that they be at least at the level of scientific and industrial progress.*

Breaking with the tradition dear to those who in Russia used to be curiously dubbed balletomanes, Massine has been careful not to lapse into pantomime. He has created this

Picasso (far right) and friends, 1917

entirely new, marvelously appealing thing, of so lyrical, human, and joyous a truth that, were the effort worthwhile, it could illumine the fearsome black sun of Dürer's "Melancholia." Jean Cocteau calls it a realistic ballet. The Cubist décor and costumes by Picasso testify to the realism of his art.

This realism—or Cubism, if you prefer—is what has most profoundly stirred the arts during the last ten years.

The décor and costumes for Parade *clearly show Picasso's concern with drawing from an object the maximum aesthetic feeling that it can convey. Artists have often sought to bring painting back to its basic elements. There is hardly anything beyond what one calls "painting" in the work of most of the Dutch, or in Chardin, or in the Impressionists.*

Picasso goes much further than all of them. You will observe this in Parade, *with an astonishment that must quickly turn into admiration. The primary problem is to translate reality. Here, however, the motif is no longer reproduced, it is merely represented; or, rather than being represented, it is suggested by a kind of analysis-synthesis embracing all its visible elements, and by something more, if this is possible—by an integral schematization that strives to reconcile contradictions by sometimes deliberately renouncing any attempt to render the immediate appearance of the object. Massine has adapted himself to the Picasso discipline in an altogether amazing way. He has identified with it, and art has thereby been enriched with charming inventions, such as the realistic gait of the horse in* Parade, *achieved by one dancer's acting as the fore feet and another as the hind feet.*

The fantastic constructions that represent those gigantic, unexpected characters, the Managers, have done anything but hinder Massine's imagination; if one may put it so, they have given him even freer rein.

In a word, Parade *will upset the ideas of many people in the audience. They are sure to be surprised, but surprised in the most agreeable way, and, being charmed, they will come to know all the grace of modern movement, of which they have never dreamed.*

A magnificent music-hall Chinese will release their imagination; the Young American Girl, as she cranks an imaginary car, will express the magic of their daily life, whose wordless rituals the Acrobat in blue and white tights celebrates with exquisite, amazing agility.

Picasso at Pompeii, 1917

(Overleaf) Managers, "Constructions" for *Parade*, by Picasso

As the curtain was rung down on the première of *Parade*, audience reactions were violent and contradictory. The ballet was a significant theatrical event, and was acclaimed as such by some intellectuals, but the majority of the public judged it irritating and inept. It was never included in the regular repertoire of the Ballets Russes.

In 1923, when Diaghilev wanted to restage *Parade*, he asked Picasso to touch up the curtain, which had been damaged by mildew. After Picasso had examined the curtain, he refused to repair it; in its present state, he said, it resembled the deteriorated frescoes of Pompeii and was much better so!

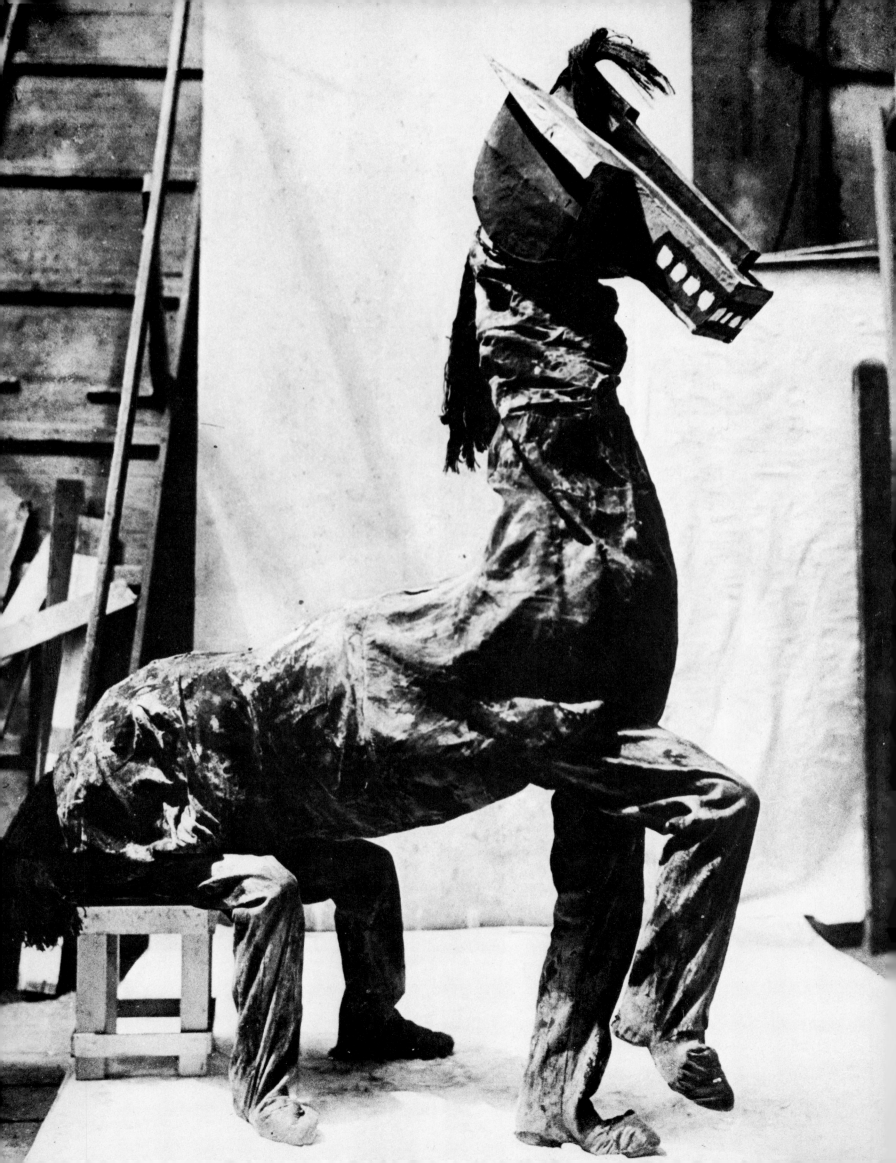

LA BOUTIQUE FANTASQUE

Ballet in one act. Music by Giacomo Rossini, arranged and orchestrated by Ottorino Respighi. Choreography by Leonide Massine. Curtain, décor, and costumes by André Derain. First performance: Alhambra Theatre, London, June 5, 1919.

The theme of *La Boutique Fantasque* was taken from the ballet *Die Puppenfee (The Fairy Dolls)*, by the German composer Josef Bayer, which had first been produced in 1888, in Vienna, and performed in St. Petersburg for the first time in 1902, at the Hermitage Theatre; in the latter production, the choreography was by Nicholas and Serge Legat, and the décor and costumes were designed by Léon Bakst. In 1903, the ballet was included in the repertoire of the Maryinsky Theatre.

This had been Bakst's first collaboration in a ballet project, and it was probably he, during his visit to Rome in the spring of 1917, who encouraged Diaghilev to stage *La Boutique Fantasque*, with the promise that he would be responsible for the mise-en-scène.

The similarity between Bakst's ideas for the new ballet and *Die Puppenfee* was obvious: he placed the action in an arcade in Naples, around 1852, whereas the set for Bayer's ballet had been the St. Petersburg Arcades, as they were at the same period.

Costume design by André Derain

Costume designs by Derain

The general plan for *La Boutique Fantasque* was worked out by Diaghilev, Bakst, and Massine, and in the fall of 1917, in Barcelona, Massine began work on the choreography. However, Diaghilev was taken up with the completion of other mise-en-scènes at the time, and he put off proceeding with the work on *La Boutique Fantasque*. It was not until two years later, in 1919, that he wrote Bakst asking him to deliver his designs with all possible speed.

On March 24, 1919, Bakst replied. In a long letter, he reproached Diaghilev as well as Massine for their silence, which had lasted a year, and he refused to finish his drawings in the too short time Diaghilev was allowing him. He made it clear that he was overburdened with commissions and that he did not have the time needed to "continue" with the décor and begin the still "missing" part—i.e., the costumes—given the fact that each of his sketches required at least one week's work, after which his pupils would have to make copies, for Bakst never entrusted his originals to the costume workrooms.

Karsavina and
Massine in
La Boutique Fantasque

Bakst ended his letter by saying:

Since you are in such a rush, order the mise-en-scène from another painter. Perhaps he will throw it together for you on the double quick. As for me, I will still have the consolation of having done something important, which in due course I will have published under the title "Boutique Fantasque," or perhaps "Naples Reverie, 1832."

It is certain that in writing this letter, the general tone of which was playful and friendly, Bakst was hoping to postpone the creation of the ballet and did not seriously suppose Diaghilev might take the mise-en-scène away from him and assign it to another painter. The sudden news that it had been entrusted to Derain upset Bakst, and was the cause of his quarrel with Diaghilev, which did not end until 1921, the year of their final collaboration.

The music for *La Boutique Fantasque* was based on a series of piano pieces that Rossini had composed to amuse his friends, whom he received every Sunday at his home in Passy, outside Paris. In 1916–17, Diaghilev had discovered the manuscripts of these pieces, most of them unpublished, in libraries and conservatories in both Italy and Paris. He had them

orchestrated by Ottorino Respighi. A brochure published in London on the occasion of the ballet's presentation there enlightens us as to the original titles of Rossini's compositions:

At these banquets there was also music. The works of young musicians were performed, and, sometimes, one by the maestro himself, who prepared for these occasions merry compositions, full of irony, most of which have unfortunately remained unpublished. The titles of these works alone suffice to show the disposition of their author. We find among them, piano pieces, entitled: "Four Hors-d'Oeuvres: Radishes, Anchovies, Gherkins and Butter, themes and variations." We discover preludes headed "Dried Figs," "Here I am, Good-Morning, Madame," "Almonds," "It is striking twelve, Good-Night, Madame." From the Albums we may take an "Anti-Dancing Valse," a "Funeral as Carnival," an "Asthmatic Study," an "Abortive Polka," a piece entitled "Ugh! Peas!," a "Convulsive Prelude," and even a Petite Valse: "Castor Oil." In the Russian vein, Rossini composed a Siberian Dance, a Slav March (which serves as prelude to "La Boutique Fantasque"), and even a Tartar Bolero, dedicated to the celebrated painter Ivanoff who lived in Rome, and to whom Rossini sends "un bacio," in his letter of June 11th, 1848.

The central number of the Ballet is dedicated by Rossini to the composer whom he admired beyond all others at this period of his life, Offenbach. The piece is entitled "Capriccio Offenbachique."

La Boutique Fantasque was a triumph in England; the only incident that threatened its brilliant future was the abrupt departure of Lydia Lopoukhova, the principal dancer in the ballet, who left the company in July, 1919. Although she was then at the height of her fame, Lopoukhova dreamed of giving up the stage and of returning to Russia.

She had no understudy in the company, and was hastily replaced by a dancer who was making her debut that season, Vera Nemtchinova. Starting with her appearance in *La Boutique Fantasque*, Nemtchinova became one of the premières danseuses of the Ballets Russes.

THE
THREE-CORNERED
HAT

———

Ballet in one act, by Martinez Sierra, after the tale by Pedro Antonio de Alarcón. Music by Manuel de Falla. Choreography by Leonide Massine. Curtain, décor, and costumes by Pablo Picasso. First performance: Alhambra Theatre, London, July 22, 1919.

In the course of the Diaghilev company's tours in Spain during the First World War, Massine "discovered" Spanish dancing, which was to have a major influence on his choreography thereafter. He was studying flamenco when, in 1918, he met a remarkable gypsy dancer, Felix Fernández, in Seville. Diaghilev immediately engaged Fernández to be Massine's instructor and to dance the leading role in an eventual Spanish ballet.

In 1919, in London, while Massine was creating the choreography for *Le Tricorne*, he was constantly assisted by Fernández, who taught him Spanish folklore and would perform for him the folk dances which Massine was using in the ballet.

Their collaboration came to a tragic end, however, for in the course of working with Massine, Fernández went insane. According to some witnesses of this tragedy, his madness was triggered by his disappointment over not finding his name on the *Tricorne* poster. Fernández was arrested by the police one night on the square before St. Martin's Church. He had smashed the red glass of the lantern that lighted the church porch, then had undressed and begun to dance.

Diaghilev,
Polounin, and Picasso
in backstage workroom,
London, 1919

Picasso and
his wife, Olga Koklova

As early as 1916, when Diaghilev was staying in Seville, he had engaged Spanish dancers for his company. But these flamenco virtuosi could make no headway in classical dance and were permanently stuck in the corps de ballet. They were Andalusian peasants, all illiterate; at Diaghilev's request, de Falla wrote out their contracts with the Ballets Russes by hand, which the dancers signed by printing their initials.

Whenever Diaghilev went to Spain for the company's current season there, he would meet de Falla, and occasionally the composer accompanied him on his travels around the country. One evening, they left Madrid or Barcelona by sleeper for some destination they were to reach the following day.

When Diaghilev woke up the next morning, he was terrified to see what he thought was a stranger in his compartment. De Falla, who was completely bald, normally wore a wig ("a superb wig," Diaghilev used to say), but during the night, as he was leaning out the train window, it had blown away and he had become quite unrecognizable.

Immediately after the triumphant première of *La Tricorne*, de Falla proposed composing a new ballet for the Diaghilev company, but the scenario he imagined so disconcerted Diaghilev that nothing came of it. Diaghilev remembered some of the details, and later told me that the action of the ballet—it was to have been full-length, lasting an entire evening—was to take place in a room with windows overlooking Vesuvius in the moonlight, and that de Falla wanted to base his score on themes from Chopin. A woman dressed in white was to mime the role of a ghost and from time to time play solos on the grand piano that was to be one of the props.

In his sketches for *Le Tricorne*, Picasso decided against the Cubist forms he had used for some of the *Parade* costumes, and created instead a dazzling spectacle in the style of traditional ballet. Yet when Diaghilev approached him later on for stage designs that did not quicken the artist's innovative imagination, Picasso sidestepped the commissions, remarking to friends that Diaghilev "would like me to do Bakst décors signed Picasso."

In the spring of 1926, the sale of the curtain Picasso had painted for *Le Tricorne* saved the life of the Ballets Russes. Diaghilev had no funds either for company salaries or for the production of new works. With Picasso's consent, he sold through Paul Rosenberg, the art dealer, the central panel of the *Tricorne* curtain and the figure paintings on the décor for *Cuadro Flamenco*.

Costume designs by Picasso

LE
CHANT DU
ROSSIGNOL

Ballet in one act by Igor Stravinsky and Leonide Massine, after the fairy tale by Hans Christian Andersen.
Music by Igor Stravinsky. Choreography by Leonide Massine. Curtain, décor, and costumes by Henri
Matisse. First performance: Théâtre National de l'Opéra, Paris, February 2, 1920. First performance of the
new version choreographed by George Balanchine: Théâtre de la Gaîté-Lyrique, Paris, June 17, 1925.

The score for this ballet was an adaptation by
Stravinsky of the music in the last two scenes of his opera *Le Rossignol*, which Diaghilev
had presented, with sets by Alexandre Benois, at the Paris Opéra in 1914.

Despite the important contributions of Stravinsky and Matisse to this production, *Le
Chant du Rossignol* was not a success, and it vanished from the Ballets Russes repertoire
the same year it was first presented. In Diaghilev's opinion, its failure was due to Massine's
hermetic choreography; he had followed the principle of imposing a rhythm on the dance
steps that was independent of the musical rhythm, having the dancers move against the
beat. The result was that, although the company had worked desperately hard for weeks,
the ballet gave the impression of having been poorly rehearsed and led people to say that
the dancers "had no ear."

When Diaghilev brought George Balanchine into the company, he was not familiar with the young artist's work as a choreographer. Actually, he had seen only a few dance numbers that Balanchine had devised for Alexandra Danilova, Tamara Gevergeyeva, Nicholas Efimov, and himself when their group had arrived from Russia and auditioned for Diaghilev. He wanted to put Balanchine to the test before entrusting him with a big production, and so made him responsible for a new choreographic version of *Le Chant du Rossignol*. In a very short time and without assistance from Diaghilev, Balanchine managed admirably the arduous task of reviving an unsuccessful ballet, and put together a production which, in first bringing to the public's attention the exceptional gifts of Alicia Markova, was one of the last great successes of the Ballets Russes.

The year that the new *Chant du Rossignol* was staged in Monte Carlo, I was present at one unforeseeable and unforgettable performance. In Massine's earlier version, the leading role of the Nightingale had been danced by Karsavina; for Alicia Markova, who was dancing the role in the Balanchine version, Matisse had designed a new costume. Made of white voile and starred with paste jewels, it fitted the little girl's body—Markova was barely fifteen at the time—as snugly as a pair of tights, and made her look touchingly virginal.

Ensembles from the original (Massine) production of *Le Chant du Rossignol*, 1920

One evening when *Rossignol* was scheduled for performance, Diaghilev learned that Markova had suddenly fallen ill and would be unable to appear. In this ballet she was irreplaceable, for only she knew the virtuoso steps of her part and only she was capable of executing them.

Diaghilev was casting about desperately for some way of keeping *Rossignol* on the evening's program when suddenly it occurred to him to have Balanchine dance Markova's role. His thought was that since Balanchine had created the choreography and knew Stravinsky's music, he could take Markova's place by improvising a new version of her part.

Having, with considerable difficulty, gotten into Markova's transparent, child-sized costume, Balanchine dreamed up for himself what he believed to be the makeup for a fairy character in the Chinese theatre, but was, in actuality, a clown's. He smeared his face with a thick layer of white grease paint and, in order to look like a bird, completed his mask with a stork's beak.

His entrance onstage was greeted by a stunned silence that gave way to shouts of laughter throughout the theatre, and, finally, to thunderous applause; people supposed they were witnessing a comedy number. But they were soon disappointed, for Balanchine was so paralyzed by the audience's response that he forgot all his own choreography and was unable to improvise a single step.

For subsequent programs that season, *Le Chant du Rossignol* was prudently struck from the announcements.

Karsavina in *Pulcinella*

——————

Sketch by Picasso

——————

Picasso and
Stravinsky, by Picasso

——————

Stravinsky, by Picasso

147

PULCINELLA

Ballet with songs, in one scene. Music by Igor Stravinsky, on themes by Giovanni Battista Pergolesi. Choreography by Leonide Massine. Décor and costumes by Pablo Picasso. First performance: Théâtre National de l'Opéra, Paris, May 15, 1920.

After searching for a long time through Italian libraries and archives, Diaghilev assembled some fragments of music by Pergolesi in a single ballet and commissioned Stravinsky to orchestrate them. The plot was based on the burlesque adventures of the commedia dell'arte hero Pulcinella. Diaghilev wanted to place the action in the ambience of a traveling actors' show, capturing the atmosphere of Neapolitan folk buffoonery of the eighteenth century.

He asked Picasso to design the set and costumes, but the sketches Picasso submitted gave rise to a violent disagreement between them.

Disregarding Diaghilev's suggestions, Picasso had executed costume designs in an 1880's style, and he envisaged the set as the interior of a theatre. The action was to take place on a small stage, in the center of the set, recessed between two wings on which spectators seated in boxes were to be painted by Picasso.

This did not correspond to Diaghilev's idea of *Pulcinella*, and he rejected the concept. Picasso was furious. In a burst of anger, he tore up his drawings for the costumes, but he spared his sketches for the set.

A few days later, having made peace with Diaghilev, he consented to prepare new designs. For the décor, he produced a drawing that represented a Neapolitan street in moonlight, and for the costumes he followed the traditional styles of the commedia dell'arte.

Sketch
for set by Picasso

Tchernicheva,
Massine,
and Nemtchinova
in *Pulcinella*

This mise-en-scène, "restrained" as it was, nonetheless proved too revolutionary for the public, and, during the 1924 Ballets Russes season in Barcelona, Diaghilev wrote me:

The Barcelonians have been scandalized by the avant-garde wit of Pulcinella. *They accept Pergolesi's music, but they find Picasso more than they can take. Mestrès [manager of the Teatro Liceo] is asking me to replace* Pulcinella *with* Cimarosiana, *our huge new success in which everything is fine—Sert's set, Cimarosa's music, and the dances!*

Diaghilev's disagreement with Picasso over the first designs for *Pulcinella* is surprising, for he immensely admired Picasso's work. He had such absolute confidence in Picasso's judgment that when he himself was disheartened by the public's lack of understanding, he used to say, "Luckily, there are ten people in this world who are able to see and understand my work. That's enough to make me happy!" And as he named these people for my benefit, Diaghilev would always begin with Picasso, but he never did manage to build the list up to ten.

One day, after lunching with Picasso at Les Gaufres, in Paris, Diaghilev watched as he walked away along the Champs-Élysées, and said to me, "Look carefully. That is how Raphael used to walk through the streets of Florence."

Diaghilev used to say also that Picasso was the only person in the world who could go to the U.S.S.R. without a passport, and he predicted that the day would come—he thought it was imminent—when the big stores would be selling a new fabric with Cubist designs, called "Picassine."

LE
ASTUZIE FEMMINILI

Opéra bouffe in three acts. Music by Domenico Cimarosa, reorchestrated by Ottorino Respighi. Choreography by Leonide Massine. Décor and costumes by José-Maria Sert. First performance: Théâtre National de l'Opéra, Paris, May 27, 1920.

CIMAROSIANA

First performance: Casino, Monte Carlo, January 8, 1924.

Diaghilev commissioned José-Maria Sert to design the mise-en-scène for the opera-ballet by Domenico Cimarosa, *Le Astuzie Femminili*, in August, 1918. Production was delayed because the Ballets Russes season in London was extended that year, and Massine did not begin to work on the staging for the singers and the dancers until February, 1920.

For three years, Cimarosa had been music master to the Empress Catherine in St. Petersburg, and the finale of his opera had been called "*Il Ballo Russo*," which led Massine to conclude his production with a choreographic divertissement. Diaghilev disagreed with this idea, and Massine describes the argument in his memoirs:

When Diaghilev came to a rehearsal and saw what I was doing, he objected strongly. He said that divertissements were entirely unnecessary and wanted me to dispense with them. I, on the other hand, insisted that a suite of dances was entirely in keeping with the pervading eighteenth-century style of the production. This led to a heated argument, but I finally persuaded Diaghilev to let me have my way and the dances stayed in. That was our first real disagreement, and the beginning of a gradual decline in our relationship and in our artistic collaboration.

The divertissement won such success in Paris and London, however, that Diaghilev decided to include it in the Ballets Russes repertoire. He supplemented it with a pas de quatre staged by Bronislava Nijinska for the "young hopefuls" of the company—Alice Nikitina, Ninette de Valois, Constantin Tcherkas, and Serge Lifar, and presented it under the title *Cimarosiana*.

Set for *Le Astuzie Femminili*, by José-Maria Sert

MY
FIRST MEETING
WITH
DIAGHILEV

It was while I was posing for my portrait that my friend Soudeikine spoke to me about the Ballets Russes and asked me to see Diaghilev on his behalf to discuss various questions concerning an eventual revival of *Salomé* at the Paris Opéra.

The evening before I was to call on Diaghilev, Soudeikine prepared a speech which he made me learn by heart and repeat in front of him. It began: "I am here on behalf of Serge Yurevich Soudeikine, who wishes to know whether . . ." This preamble was followed by several responses that I was to give to the questions Diaghilev would presumably ask me.

On February 27, 1921, at ten in the morning, I arrived at the Hôtel Scribe, which was

Serge Soudeikine portrait of Boris Kochno

the address Soudeikine had given me, and asked to see M. de Diaghilev. The concierge replied that Diaghilev had not lived at the hotel for years, but that most likely I would find him at the Continental.

Some minutes later, I repeated my question at the reception desk of the Hôtel Continental. The clerk consulted the clock in the lobby; then, without either looking at me or asking my name, he told me the number of Diaghilev's room.

Later I learned that on that particular day Diaghilev, who never received strangers, was expecting a visit from someone who was to arrive at the hotel between ten and ten-fifteen, and he had left instructions that this person should be sent up to his room without being announced. The expected caller did not come or was late, and it was I who took his place.

Diaghilev's valet opened the door, inquired as to the purpose of my call, and asked me to wait. I was marking time in the corridor, rereading Soudeikine's memorandum, not a word of which I understood, and trying in vain to recall his instructions, when Diaghilev appeared. He walked quickly toward me and, giving me no time to apologize for disturbing him, asked me to excuse him for having made me wait. As he spoke, he led me to the Turkish salon on the main floor of the hotel, where, seated in front of him, I was able to launch into my monologue: "I am here on behalf of Serge Yurevich . . ."

I came to the end of my first speech. There was nothing more I could say until Diaghilev asked me a question. I had learned only answers.

Diaghilev did not say a word. He had not heard my speech. He was chewing his tongue, as was his habit when thinking hard about something.

Abruptly, as if roused from a deep sleep, he broke the silence. "How old are you?" he asked.

"I have just turned seventeen."

This reply, like all the others that were to follow, had not been foreseen by Soudeikine. Diaghilev led me on to talk about my family, about the poetry I was then writing, about when I had left Moscow, and especially about the revolution in Russia. I no longer remember the sequence of our conversation; I only know that the word "Russia" figured constantly in his questions. To him, who had left St. Petersburg in 1914, I was someone who "had just arrived from there."

At the beginning of my tale, his eyes followed me attentively; then he dropped his monocle, and a faraway expression came into his eyes. He was looking over my head, as if, beyond me, he were seeing a snow-covered landscape, a forgotten landscape.

I left the Turkish salon at one o'clock. Diaghilev accompanied me to the door and said to me, "We will meet again."

Early in March, some days after my call at the Hôtel Continental, in the capacity of Diaghilev's personal secretary I left with him and Stravinsky for Spain, where the 1921 Ballets Russes season was scheduled to open.

CHOUT
(LE BOUFFON)

Russian legend in six scenes. Music by Serge Prokofiev. Choreography by Michel Larionov and Tadeo Slavinsky. Curtain, décor, and costumes by Larionov. First performance: Théâtre de la Gaîté-Lyrique, Paris, May 17, 1921.

Massine had been with the Ballets Russes as premier danseur and then as choreographer since 1914. In January, 1921, for personal reasons, he suddenly left the Diaghilev group. Several dancers from the company followed him, and with them he formed a new company which made its debut that same year in Latin America.

Although Massine was replaced in the leading roles of the company's repertoire by two young dancers, Léon Woizikowski and Stanislas Idzikowski, the Diaghilev enterprise was left, suddenly, without a choreographer.

At the time of Massine's departure, *Chout* headed the list of forthcoming Diaghilev productions. The ballet score, commissioned from Prokofiev in 1915, had long since been completed, as had Larionov's designs for the sets and costumes.

Costume design for *Chout*, by Larionov

Ansermet,
Diaghilev,
Stravinsky,
Prokofiev,
in London, 1921

159

Diaghilev wished to present this ballet as quickly as possible and, remembering that Larionov had shared in Massine's early choreographic efforts, asked him to act as "choreographic adviser" to one of the company's dancers, Tadeo Slavinsky, whom he assigned to devise the dances for *Chout*. Without bothering his head over Slavinsky's creative abilities, Diaghilev appointed him to be the interpreter of Larionov's theatrical ideas; that is, he was to translate these ideas into a dance idiom and act as intermediary between Larionov and the dancers.

On March 15, 1921, in anticipation of the *Chout* production, Larionov signed a contract whereby he agreed to "join the ballet company of Diaghilev for a period of three months, to act as artistic director and to collaborate with the choreographer and dancers."

On March 24, Larionov wrote to Diaghilev from Hendaye, where he was waiting for his Spanish visa in order to join the company in Madrid and begin work with Slavinsky:

I've studied Chout *and learned it by heart. I've bought a big new notebook and am busy working out entrances and dance figures. The whole of* Chout *is in my head, ready to be staged. It's exhausting to keep it there!*

Sketches for sets by Larionov

Slavinsky,
by Juan Gris

Slavinsky and
Lydia Sokolova
in *Chout*

Nijinska
in *Chout*, 1922

Portrait of
Prokofiev by Henri
Matisse, 1921

I'm changing the scenario because, on the whole, it is too sketchy and not very precise. Furthermore, Prokofiev constantly indicates the movements of a given character but then brings a second onstage and forgets the first. The result is that characters keep piling up onstage—but doing what one can't exactly tell. Yet the scenario never calls for them to go offstage. They couldn't, for that matter, because ten or fifteen measures later they encounter each other again. [Larionov seems to have forgotten that they must dance!] *So, for all the time that they must remain onstage I have regrouped them and worked out their positions in greater detail.*

This attempt at a collaboration between Slavinsky and Larionov had no sequel. *Chout* was considered more pantomime than ballet, and it put Paris audiences off because there was no harmony between Prokofiev's limpid, cool music and Larionov's aggressive use of folk motifs in his sets and his Constructivist costumes.

Before the dress rehearsal of *Chout* in Paris, Diaghilev had to threaten the dancers with fines to persuade them to appear onstage in costumes that were so heavy and cumbersome that they interfered with the movements of the dance.

The first London performance of *Chout*, which took place June 8, 1921, at the Princess Theatre, was preceded by a small incident. Diaghilev wanted to present the new ballet to some prominent Londoners at a preview, and accordingly invited them to the theatre for one of the last rehearsals. Prokofiev was conducting; he considered it a working rehearsal and, wishing to be more comfortable, he ignored the presence of the spectators and removed his jacket. Immediately, several elderly ladies from London high society who were sitting in the first row of the orchestra rose, scandalized, to their feet and, followed by their escorts, left the theatre. It was a signal for all Diaghilev's invited guests to depart.

Chout was included in the company's repertoire for the last time during the Paris season of June, 1922, at the Théâtre Mogador. The principal role of the Buffoon, which had been created by Slavinsky, was danced by Bronislava Nijinska.

CUADRO FLAMENCO

Suite of Andalusian dances. Décor and costumes by Pablo Picasso. First performance: Théâtre de la Gaîté-Lyrique, Paris, May 17, 1921.

In the spring of 1921, during the Ballets Russes season in Madrid, Diaghilev handed over responsibility for the performances to the company's regisseur, Serge Grigoriev, and with Stravinsky and me he took off for Seville "on vacation." The vacation consisted of day-long work sessions with Stravinsky on the Tchaikovsky score for *The Sleeping Beauty* and night-long tours of the "singing and dancing" cabarets of La Triana and other working-class sections of the city.

Diaghilev had given proof of his admiration for flamenco singing and dancing by

Diaghilev and Stravinsky, Seville, 1921

producing *Le Tricorne* in 1919. In 1924, he wrote to me from Barcelona:

A pity you are not here to see the cabarets. My goddesses, Macarona and Carnichona, are dancing at one of them—and they're amazing, wonderful. The whole company was at the cabaret with me, and the applause very nearly brought down the roof. There is one other famous cabaret here, but I haven't been to it yet because the dancing starts at three in the morning.

In 1921, after his break with Massine, Diaghilev could not hope to put on more than one new ballet with a novice choreographer like Slavinsky, and this would not be enough for his next Paris season. It was while he was applauding the flamenco artists in Seville's cabarets that he had the idea of including them in the Ballets Russes program.

This decided, Diaghilev attended all the cabaret shows in Seville and began to choose the flamenco dancers and singers to make up a company.

A friend of Diaghilev's, the Spanish painter José Lafita, and his business manager, Randolfo Barocchi, were charged with the duty of assembling all the contestants, who followed each other night after night on the stage of a cabaret room closed to the public.

Diaghilev's task was complicated by the fact that most of these artists had not the slightest intention of signing contracts or of leaving Spain; they came for the pleasure of being applauded.

While each contestant waited for his turn to appear before Diaghilev, he was allowed to drink what he wanted and in whatever quantity. I saw several of the artists quite incapable, when the moment came, of getting to their feet to walk to the stage. Some competitors came back several nights in a row without our ever discovering their artistic qualifications.

Maria Dalbaicin

One day while driving through the outskirts of Seville in the company of Barocchi and myself, Diaghilev was struck by the beauty of a young gypsy he noticed among the passers-by. He ordered the cab to stop, talked with the young stranger, learned that she was a dancer and that she had just arrived from the nethermost regions of Andalusia to make her Seville debut. Diaghilev instantly offered her an engagement with his company, and for her appearance in *Cuadro Flamenco* he substituted for her name, Pepita Ramoje, the name of Maria Dalbaicin.

When he got several Spanish artists to promise that they would join his company, Diaghilev, who had to leave Seville, made Barocchi responsible for persuading them to sign contracts. Soon, either in Monte Carlo or in Paris, he began to receive daily wires from Barocchi, of which these are typical:

SEVILLE, APRIL 27. ATTITUDE RAMIREZ AND MACARONA UNBELIEVABLE. WILL NOT DISCUSS MONEY. . . . MADNESS TO COUNT ON THEM FOR AT LAST MOMENT WILL NOT COME. MALENA ASKING HUNDRED PESETAS A DAY. VEZ WITH PERFORMING HUSBAND TWO HUNDRED. ESTAMPILLO FORTY. ALL DISCUSSION OF FEES USELESS.

SEVILLE, APRIL 27. HAVE SPENT ENTIRE EVENING WITH MACARONA AND RAMIREZ. THEY DECIDED FINALLY TO TELL ME THEIR FEE TOMORROW, THEREFORE AM SLIGHTLY HOPEFUL. DO NOTHING BUT EMBRACE THEM ENTIRE TIME.

SEVILLE, APRIL 28. MACARONA ASKING MINIMUM ONE MONTH CONTRACT THREE THOUSAND PESETAS. . . . RAMIREZ THOUSAND FIVE HUNDRED . . . ESSENTIAL THEY LEAVE WITH ME. . . . IF YOU APPROVE, WIRE TRAVEL ADVANCES ALSO MONEY FOR PANTS SHOES FOR RAMIREZ.

SEVILLE, APRIL 28. RAMIREZ NOW INSISTING ON IDENTICAL TERMS MACARONA.

Robert Delaunay,
Boris Kochno, Stravinsky,
Sonia Delaunay,
Diaghilev,
Manuel de Falla,
and Randolfo Barocchi,
Madrid, 1921

Maria Dalbaicin

SEVILLE, MAY 3. TRYING ONE SOLID WEEK ENGAGE MANOLO CALLED HUELVANO WHO DECLINES EVEN THOUSAND FIVE HUNDRED PESETAS A MONTH. HUSBAND MINARITA MAGNIFICENT PERFORMER GREAT FRIEND MANOLO BUT ALSO UNABLE PERSUADE HIM SIGN.

SEVILLE, MAY 7. MINARITA AND VEZ [SINGERS] DO NOT DANCE. PREFER VEZ BECAUSE PRETTIER BETTER VOICE BUT INSISTS SINGING SONGS WITH ORCHESTRA PLUS SIX THOUSAND PESETAS A MONTH. . . . RAMIREZ HAS LOST WITS. REFUSES TO SIGN UNLESS WE ENGAGE ROSARIO WHO WILL NOT COME WITHOUT AUNT OR MACARONA OR MALENA, WHO NOW ASKING SIX THOUSAND WITH HUSBAND PERFORMER.

MADRID, MAY 8. RED DANCER REFUSED FLATLY BEFORE POLICE AND TOVAR [THE DUKE OF TOVAR, THEN GOVERNOR OF MADRID] TO LEAVE BEFORE TUESDAY NIGHT. NASTY DISPOSITION ERGO UNWISE INSIST.

And the final wire from Madrid, on which Diaghilev scrawled "Spanish artists!":

MADRID, MAY 10. ABSOLUTELY INDISPENSABLE YOU MEET ME STATION THURSDAY WITH ADDRESS CHEAP PENSION AND BUS TRANSPORTATION FOR ENTIRE FLOCK FOR THEY ALL REPEAT ALL DOTTY. BAROCCHI.

In the end, after three weeks of palaver with Barocchi, only Estampillo and La Minarita agreed to come to Paris. Barocchi was obliged to put Diaghilev's Spanish company together haphazardly and at the last moment. As for the two "phenomena" who created a sensation in *Cuadro Flamenco* both in Paris and London—"*Mate el sin pies*," a legless beggar who used to roam the streets of Seville in a box on wheels parodying the running of the bulls, and Gabrielita del Garrotín, a dwarf and a remarkable dancer—Diaghilev had discovered and hired them before he left Spain.

It had been Diaghilev's intention to commission Juan Gris to design the décor and costumes for *Cuadro Flamenco*, and when he returned to Paris from Seville, he asked Picasso's opinion. Picasso approved the idea, but when Diaghilev went back to his studio, he found all the sketches for the ballet already done by Picasso himself.

For the décor, Picasso adapted an earlier idea for a set he had prepared in 1920 for *Pulcinella*; the costumes he designed after the traditional garb of flamenco dancers.

The day after the première at the Princess Theatre, in London, Diaghilev received a message from the Spanish Ambassador, Merry del Val, asking that *Cuadro Flamenco* be withdrawn because, in his opinion, it ridiculed and dishonored his country, which he officially represented in Great Britain.

The Ambassador's request vexed and embarrassed Diaghilev, the more so because *Cuadro Flamenco* was scheduled to be presented again that same day and no other ballet in the repertoire was in shape to replace it. He decided to give it one last time and to substitute something else the following night. As he came into the theatre and the curtain was going up on *Cuadro Flamenco*, Diaghilev learned that the King of Spain, Alfonso XIII, who had just arrived in London incognito, was in the theatre in the company of friends.

At the end of the Spanish ballet, we saw the King applauding. The next morning, Diaghilev received a second note from Merry del Val. The Ambassador wrote that, knowing how greatly it would please His Majesty to see a portion of *Cuadro Flamenco* performed for his guests, he was requesting Diaghilev to authorize Maria Dalbaicin to dance, accompanied by her guitarists, that same evening at a reception to be given by the Spanish Embassy.

Set for *Cuadro Flamenco*

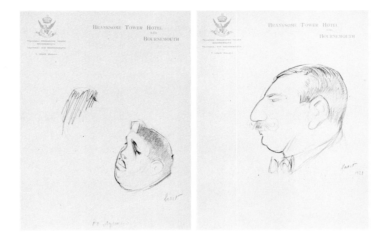

THE
SLEEPING BEAUTY

Ballet in five scenes, after the Perrault fairy tale. Music by Peter Ilyich Tchaikovsky, partially reorchestrated by Igor Stravinsky. Choreography by Marius Petipa, restored by Nicholas Sergeyev and completed by Bronislava Nijinska. Décor and costumes by Léon Bakst. First performance: Alhambra Theatre, London, November 2, 1921.

After Massine's departure from the Ballets Russes, Diaghilev decided to replace the productions that had been planned for the forthcoming season with the revival of one of the classical ballet masterpieces unknown in Europe—*The Sleeping Beauty*. He asked Sergeyev, who had formerly been the regisseur of the Maryinsky Theatre, to restore the Petipa choreography, and asked Stravinsky to reorchestrate part of Tchaikovsky's score. Diaghilev wanted to entrust the mise-en-scène to Alexandre Benois, but he could not persuade Benois to leave Russia. So, after his reconciliation with Léon Bakst, whom he had not seen since the *Boutique Fantasque* incident, he commissioned Bakst to design the sets and costumes for his new production.

The uncut version of the Petipa work called for a large company, and Diaghilev's first concern was to find new dancers. He rounded out the corps de ballet with students from London and Paris dancing schools. He decided that he would have to engage his leading dancers from the Imperial Theatres, for he had discovered in the course of the first rehearsals of *Sleeping Beauty* that in dancing Massine's modern choreography the company had lost the technique and the purity of style of classical ballet. His efforts to contact dancers in Russia were unsuccessful, so he engaged soloists from the Imperial Theatres who were living in Europe as refugees: Vera Trefilova, Lubov Egorova, Felia Doubrovska, Ludmila Schollar, Pierre Vladimirov, Anatole Vilzak.

BALLET

IN FIVE SCENES

AFTER PERRAULT'S TALE

The Sleeping Princess

(LA BELLE AU BOIS DORMANT)

The entire production by M. Leon Bakst.

MUSIC BY TCHAIKOVSKY

Orchestration revised by ~~~~~~~~~~

Prelude of 3rd Scene

~~Entr'acte between Scenes 1 and 2~~ and Aurora's Variation in Scene 3
orchestrated by IGOR STRAVINSKY.

Choreography by MARIUS PETIPA.

Reproduced by M. SERGUEÏEFF,
Regisseur-en-chef of the Imperial Opera, Petrograd.

The Action-Scenes, Hunting Dances in Scene 3,
Aurora's Variation in the same scene, and tales
of Bluebeard, Sheherazade, and Innocent Ivan,
produced by LA NIJINSKA

~~Curtain, Scenery, Costumes and Properties by LEON BAKST~~

Curtain painted by M. OUDOT.

Scenes 1 2 4 and 5 painted by O. ALLEGRI.
Scene 3 painted by MR. and MRS. POLUNIN.
The Growing Forest painted by M. CHEVALLIER.

Costumes executed by
M. PIERRE PITOEFF, MRS. LOVAT FRASER, and LA MAISON MEULLE.

Wigs by PONTET.   Shoes by CRAIT and GAMBA

le nom de Tchaïkovsky plus grand que les noms de Bakst et Stravinsky

plus grand

Sketches for *The Sleeping Beauty*, by Bakst

For the role of the fairy Carabosse, Diaghilev engaged Carlotta Brianza, who in 1890 had created the role of the Princess Aurora. At the hundredth performance, the role of Carabosse was danced by Maestro Cecchetti, who had danced the Bluebird when the ballet was first performed in Russia.

Wishing to conform to the traditions of the Maryinsky, Diaghilev went to Padua to see the composer Riccardo Drigo, who had studied the score with Tchaikovsky and conducted the orchestra at the St. Petersburg première of *The Sleeping Beauty* in 1890. Diaghilev questioned Drigo about this early collaboration, but Drigo, by then very old, seemed to have lost all recollection of it.

In September, 1921, Diaghilev learned that Olga Spessivtzeva had arrived in Latvia from Russia. He asked a theatrical agent in Riga to send him Spessivtzeva's address, and in due course received a letter that said:

I've just now unearthed Spessivtzeva; she is here en route to Italy. Poor girl, the Bolsheviks let her out so that she could have her health seen to, but they've given her no money for the necessary care. She's living here in a garret, with her mother.

Diaghilev had never seen Spessivtzeva perform, but he knew her reputation as a great dancer. After long negotiations, he managed to engage her and had her come to London, where I saw her for the first time during a rehearsal.

When I came into the studio with Diaghilev, Spessivtzeva was working at the barre. Among the other dancers, all of whom were wearing black tunics, the required costume for rehearsals, she appeared quite strange, for she was wearing a full yellow tutu and her long, unbraided hair fell down her back. She began to rehearse Aurora's variation. The others, who were working all over the room, stopped one by one and stood motionless, watching her dance. Smiling, she moved with an extraordinary serenity and ease, and the virtuoso steps she was executing seemed simple and natural. She never had to reach for balance; she seemed to be sustained by an invisible thread. At the end of the variation, there was a long, admiring silence, and then the room exploded into applause—company rules forbade it, but that day it was Diaghilev himself who first gave the signal.

Spessivtzeva, Lopoukhova, and Bakst

———

Spessivtzeva in *The Sleeping Beauty*

That same autumn, Diaghilev received word from Bronislava Nijinska, Vaslav's sister, who had arrived in Vienna. She had come on from Kiev, where she had founded a school of dance, and now she asked Diaghilev to engage her as choreographer. In August, Diaghilev sent Walter Nouvel, an old friend who now was also business manager of the Ballets Russes, to Austria. Nouvel kept him informed by letter of his discussions with Nijinska. After describing his first meeting with her, he wrote: "I wonder whether she is not the dream choreographer you need." By September, Nijinska was in London, where she revised Petipa's choreography and added several new numbers to the ballet.

In 1929, Diaghilev described *The Sleeping Beauty* dress rehearsal:

The dress rehearsal was a disaster. The stage machinery did not work; the trees in the enchanted woods did not sprout; the backdrop shifts did not come off; the tulle skirts got tangled in the flats. The première suffered accordingly, and the financial losses that ensued were incalculable. By staging this ballet, I very nearly killed off my theatrical venture abroad.

This misadventure taught me a lesson. I see in it an occult hint—for our whole life is full of these warnings—which is that it is not my business and it is not up to me to concern myself with reviving the triumphs of days gone by.

Diaghilev did not mention here that at the dress rehearsal Spessivtzeva, whose first appearance was awaited as a great theatrical event, slipped and fell to the floor just as she was commencing her first variation.

In the course of that London season, an incident which could have been tragic caused Diaghilev to pass a night of sleepless anguish.

After endless negotiations with Vera Trefilova, who in Russia was one of the most celebrated interpreters of the role of the Princess Aurora, Diaghilev had succeeded in adding her to his company, and he had announced the date of her debut at the Alhambra.

On the eve of this performance, Diaghilev was awakened in the middle of the night by a violent pounding on his door. There stood a Hotel Savoy porter, as pale and stammering as if he had just seen a ghost. The man handed Diaghilev a letter from Trefilova. It said:

If you do not release me from my contract, which I signed all unawares and which requires me to appear in The Sleeping Beauty *at my age [Trefilova was forty-six], at a time when I have lost all technical skill, this very night I will kill myself and you shall be responsible for my death. . . .*

Diaghilev answered neither Trefilova's letter nor her incessant telephone calls, and

Sketch for *The Sleeping Beauty*, by Bakst

the next evening, looking as if she were sixteen, she triumphed in the role of Aurora.

The Sleeping Beauty was given a hundred and fifteen performances at the Alhambra, and yet from the outset this long season was catastrophic. Habitually, the British press accused the Ballets Russes of being too advanced for the public's comprehension; on this occasion, it reproached Diaghilev for being incapable of creating new ballets. The production was compared to provincial Christmas pantomime shows, and Tchaikovsky's score was likened to circus music. At the last performance, with Eugene Goossens conducting, the wind instruments were playing the final mazurka when the brasses struck up with "*Ach, du lieber Augustin . . .*"

The general public subscribed to the verdict of the press. Audiences had been accustomed by earlier Diaghilev seasons to programs that included three different ballets. Now they were bored to see the same characters reappear throughout an entire evening; they found the production monotonous.

Every morning, Bakst used to come to see Diaghilev at the Savoy and suggest new ideas for enlivening or updating the production. One day, he persuaded Diaghilev to add a *tableau vivant* to the ballet; the sleeping château was to be peopled with extras and animals who, as Bakst visualized it, would remain motionless, not stirring until the moment when Beauty awakes. However, that day there was no time for a rehearsal, and at the performance the dogs held on leash by the valets frisked about and yelped, the poultry flapped and struggled in the hands of the scullery boys, while the cats leaped from the laps of the court ladies and took off, meowing, into the wings. . . . This venture knew no tomorrow.

Another of Bakst's numerous ideas was to replace the musical entr'acte with a comic skit, which was to be written by George Bernard Shaw and acted in front of the curtain by Lopoukhova and Idzikowski.

Although *The Sleeping Beauty* was a failure, more than any other ballet Diaghilev

Costume design for
The Sleeping Beauty,
by Bakst

———

Walter Nouvel,
by Bakst

presented it created in London a public of new ballet lovers, a public of young enthusiasts who learned to appreciate the technical qualities of a performance and who came back to the theatre every evening. But they could afford only the cheap seats, and their support was not enough to save the enterprise from financial disaster.

Diaghilev left London in debt by eleven thousand pounds to Sir Oswald Stoll, manager of the Alhambra, who had advanced the money to stage the production of *The Sleeping Beauty*. At the end of the season, Sir Oswald took legal action to have the ballet's properties sequestered.

Worried about what the Paris public's verdict on the ballet would be—it was scheduled to be presented at the Opéra—Bakst, who had returned to Paris from London, on December 12, 1921, sent Diaghilev a long list of fresh changes. Among them:

. . . in Paris, the posters for Sleeping Beauty *should read "fairy ballet." If the snobs were informed that the Ballets Russes was staging a* fairy ballet, *they would be touched and would proclaim it high time to produce some marvelous fairies (which is true!). Whereas, were one to try to hide the ass's ears (the fairy ballet's ears, that is) in a sack by calling our production simply a ballet, people would shout, "No, this is no ballet, this is just another 'Châtelet,' only done somewhat better"—and it would be the end of us!*

Keep up your spirits. . . . Strange as it may seem, our best classical ballets were fairy plays, and it strikes me that this is what they used to be called.

Scenes from *The Sleeping Beauty*, 1921

Royal Opera House

COVENT GARDEN

Mr. Serge Diaghileff

requests the honour of the Company of

_____

to assist at the Final Rehearsal on

MONDAY, JULY 15th, at noon

at the

ROYAL OPERA HOUSE, COVENT GARDEN

of

IGOR STRAVINSKY'S Music

for the

"RENARD"

Previous to its first presentation in England

and the

CONCERTO for Piano

by

IGOR MARKEVITCH

Played by the Composer and the
COVENT GARDEN ORCHESTRA

12 Noon, Monday, July 15th   Cocktails 1 p.m.

LE RENARD

Ballet-burlesque, with songs. Words and music by Igor Stravinsky. Choreography by Bronislava Nijinska. Décor and costumes by Michel Larionov. First performance: Théâtre National de l'Opéra, Paris, May 18, 1922.

Diaghilev ordered the set for *Renard* from Serge Soudeikine, who, since the Russian Revolution, had been living in Paris, where he had become the principal stage designer for Nikita Baliev's *Chauve Souris*. However, from their very first conversation about *Renard*, the relationship between the two men was complicated. Disappointed in the sketches Soudeikine had prepared for this ballet, Diaghilev decided to abandon their collaboration, and he took as his pretext the working conditions Soudeikine stipulated.

Costume design by Michel Larionov

178

Diaghilev, by Larionov

Costume design by
Larionov for 1922 production
of *Le Renard*

Costume design by
Larionov for Lifar's version
of *Le Renard*, 1929

Nijinska, 1924

Sketch for *Le Renard*
set, by Diaghilev

Scene from *Le Renard*, 1922

Diaghilev, by Larionov

Nicholas Efimov
and Woizikowski in
Le Renard, 1929

Soudeikine said, in effect, that he had resolved to work in the theatre henceforth only if he were entrusted with the entire production. Had Diaghilev agreed, it would have compromised the credits due other painters whose names might appear alongside Soudeikine's in the Ballets Russes programs.

Although the connection between the two men was broken, Diaghilev maintained friendly relations with Soudeikine's wife, Vera Arturovna, who later became Mme. Stravinsky. Vera's sculpturesque beauty had led Diaghilev to ask her to mime the role of the Queen in his 1921 London production of *The Sleeping Beauty*, and later Mme. Soudeikine organized a sewing workshop that made numerous costumes for the Ballets Russes.

Stravinsky, 1922

After the disagreement with Soudeikine, Diaghilev commissioned Michel Larionov to design the *Renard* set, and took an active part in the work. A rough sketch that Diaghilev drew in a notebook now in my possession was the basis of Larionov's décor and testifies to their close collaboration.

Renard was Nijinska's first complete choreography for the Ballets Russes, and the ballet's success decided Diaghilev to engage her as the company's permanent choreographer. In his *Souvenirs et Commentaires* Stravinsky says of Nijinska: "Her choreography for the original productions of *Le Renard* (1922) and of *Les Noces* (1923) pleased me more than any other of my works performed by the Diaghilev company."

Renard was given only in 1922. In 1929, Diaghilev planned to revive it, but by then Nijinska was no longer connected with the company and the dancers did not remember her choreography. Since Diaghilev was eager to give Serge Lifar a chance to become a choreographer, he turned over to him the staging of a new version. Diaghilev insisted that Lifar use acrobats in the ballet, and he arranged for Larionov to supervise the choreography.

The new version of *Le Renard* was first performed at the Théâtre Sarah Bernhardt, in Paris, on May 21, 1929.

On July 15, 1929, the evening before its first London showing, Diaghilev organized a symphonic concert at Covent Garden at which the Stravinsky ballet score was performed, together with a concerto by Igor Markevich, with the composer at the piano. Markevich was Diaghilev's last disciple.

AURORA'S WEDDING

Classical ballet by Marius Petipa. Music by Peter Ilyich Tchaikovsky. Choreography by Marius Petipa, supplemented by dances composed by Bronislava Nijinska. Décor and costumes by Alexandre Benois and Nathalie Gontcharova. First performance: Théâtre National de l'Opéra, Paris, May 18, 1922.

During *The Sleeping Beauty* season in London, Diaghilev signed a contract with the director of the Paris Opéra, Jacques Rouché, for a series of performances by the Ballets Russes to be given in May, 1922. In addition to the old repertoire, Diaghilev agreed to present the complete version of *Sleeping Beauty* and to produce two new works by Stravinsky.

In anticipation of the Paris performances, Rouché sent the Opéra's stage manager to London to study at first hand, in the Alhambra Theatre, the scene-shifting the Bakst sets required. However, when the London season ended so disastrously, with the scenery and costumes for *Sleeping Beauty* sequestered by the Alhambra's manager, Sir Oswald Stoll, it was impossible for Diaghilev to fulfill his Paris commitments. On the eve of the Monte Carlo season, which preceded the one in Paris, Diaghilev had virtually no company, because after the English season he had been obliged to give all his dancers an indefinite leave of absence.

He warned Rouché of these difficulties, and on April 26 he received the following letter:

Dear Friend:

The information you gave me yesterday about The Sleeping Beauty *is insufficient, and I would be grateful if you were to give me complete details.*

Our contract stipulates that, in addition to the standard repertoire, the new works will be The Sleeping Beauty *and M. Stravinsky's* Noces Villageoises *and* Mavra.

You would like to substitute Renard *for* Noces Villageoises. *There is no problem on this point. But in place of* The Sleeping Beauty, *which is a big, evening-long ballet, you propose giving me a fragment of the work,* The Marriage of the Sleeping Beauty.

*You understand how box-office receipts can be affected by a one-acter's being inserted in a program of old ballets as the substitute for a brilliant production composed of a single, entirely new work. I had counted on a profitable success—*The Sleeping Beauty *being already known here thanks to the stir its numerous London performances have created, together with* *its magnificent production, the several sets and the costumes created by Bakst, and the quality of the dancers.*

You have neglected to tell me what décor and costumes you will use in presenting the excerpt. Will Bakst be collaborating on them? If, to my great regret and despite your wishes and mine, Mlle. Spessivtzeva cannot come to Paris, her absence would not be sufficient cause for canceling the ballet altogether. In October, you yourself told me you would have a number of stars perform in the ballet and that in Paris you would perhaps ask me for Mlle. Zambelli.

The solution you suggest presents nothing but problems: more stars, more sets, more stage designs. Therefore, I must ask for clarification of your new program. What artist will execute the sets and costumes for The Marriage of the Sleeping Beauty? *Lastly, who will the members of the company be?*

However, Rouché's friendship with Diaghilev and his confidence in him made it easy for them to arrive at a new understanding. Rouché's reply to a letter that Diaghilev had written in 1920, the contents of which one can infer, attests to their previous friendly relationship:

Dear M. de Diaghilev:

As I have told you, there is nothing the director can do at this point, but the friend does not wish to leave you in difficulties. Here is the check. . . .

Cordially,
J. Rouché

In the end, Diaghilev's agreement with Rouché was that he would present only the last scene of *The Sleeping Beauty*, under the title *Aurora's Wedding*; and would replace *Noces Villageoises*—that is, *Les Noces*—with *Renard* and *Mavra*.

For *Aurora's Wedding* Diaghilev replaced Bakst's décor and costumes with Benois's mise-en-scène for *Le Pavillon d'Armide,* and he ordered some supplementary costume designs from Nathalie Gontcharova.

During the performances of this ballet at the Opéra and the Théâtre Mogador in 1922, the shortage of premiers danseurs in the company made it necessary for Nijinska to appear in four different roles.

MAVRA

Opéra bouffe, after a poem by Alexander Pushkin. Book by Boris Kochno. Music by Igor Stravinsky. Décor and costumes by Léopold Survage. First performance: Théâtre National de l'Opéra, Paris, June 3, 1922.

In 1921, Diaghilev rediscovered the passion for opera he had had as a young man. The temporary lack of an outstanding choreographer and dancers in his company was, very likely, one reason for his turning again to lyric theatre.

During our stay in Seville and Madrid that spring, Diaghilev used to discuss with Stravinsky the forthcoming production of *The Sleeping Beauty* and play a four-hand arrangement of the Tchaikovsky score with him. It was then that he got the idea of rounding out the next year's programs with a curtain raiser and, with this in view, asked Stravinsky to compose a short chamber opera.

We searched among the Russian classics for a scenario with only a few characters, and finally settled on a satiric poem by Pushkin, *A Small House in Kolomna*. Stravinsky's opéra

bouffe, for which Diaghilev asked me to write the lyrics, was first entitled *La Cuisinière* and, finally, *Mavra*.

On January 11, 1922, Stravinsky wrote to Diaghilev from Biarritz, where he was working on the score: "*Mavra* seems to me the best thing I've done."

In Spain, while the *Mavra* project was being developed, Stravinsky was simultaneously considering composing an opera in several acts on the *Barber of Seville* theme. He asked me to write the libretto, setting the action in our own period, and he proposed to integrate into his score the improvisations of the Andalusian guitarists whom he had admired in the *cuadros flamencos* of the Seville cabarets.

Stravinsky intended his *Barber of Seville* for a season of opera that Diaghilev was then planning. For the same season, Diaghilev wanted to commission Prokofiev to write a comic opera based on Mikhail Lermontov's "The Tambov Treasurer's Wife."

The first public audition of *Mavra*, with Stravinsky at the piano, took place May 29, 1922, at a concert of Russian music that Diaghilev arranged for his friends in Paris and presented in the public rooms of the Hôtel Continental.

That evening it was a triumphant success, whereas a few days later its performance at

Set for *Mavra*, by Léopold Survage

the Opéra was a failure. *Mavra* was not at all suited to the monumental proportions of the Théâtre National; alone on the immense stage, the four soloists who made up the entire cast of this musical farce were lost. Furthermore, Stravinsky's score, which reflected the influence of nineteenth-century classical Russian music, had a subtlety and a spare orchestration that disappointed the Paris music-goers, who considered it insubstantial. At the première of *Mavra*, the first duet, which had been received with an ovation at the Continental, met with no response at all from the Opéra audience; one might have supposed that the theatre was empty. After a moment of attentive silence, people began to stir and speak to one another; if the house lights had not been turned up and the curtain lowered to signal the intermission, one would scarcely have noticed that the performance was over.

On his return to Biarritz, where he was living at the time, Stravinsky wrote to me on August 6, 1922:

> . . . *If only listeners could hear my music as I write it, I think they would say many fewer foolish things about it. I must confess that in these last years I mostly hear only ineptitudes about the qualities of my music, of which I am entirely aware, but no one (literally, no one) speaks of its lacunae, which for me are often a source of torment. It relegates me to an immense solitude that at times is very painful.*

The joint production that Diaghilev had planned for *Mavra* and *The Sleeping Beauty* but could not in fact carry out accounts for the misunderstanding that arose between him and Bakst.

Only after he had commissioned the sets for both works from Bakst did Diaghilev realize that it would be impossible to combine them in a single program, for the uncut version of the Tchaikovsky ballet ran a full evening.

Forced to postpone *Mavra*, Diaghilev wanted to avoid Bakst's working on the production that would immediately follow *Sleeping Beauty*. He broke his contract with Bakst, paying him the stipulated forfeit, and commissioned Survage to undertake the décor for *Mavra*.

This incident caused a definitive rupture in the friendly relations between the two men. But in 1924, in London, I saw Diaghilev weep when he heard of Bakst's death.

LES NOCES

Choreographic Russian scenes, in four acts without intermission. Words and music by Igor Stravinsky. Choreography by Bronislava Nijinska. Décor and costumes by Nathalie Gontcharova. First performance: Théâtre de la Gaîté-Lyrique, Paris, June 13, 1923.

In 1913, immediately after the Ballets Russes's creation of *Le Sacre du Printemps*, Diaghilev had asked Stravinsky to compose the score for *Les Noces*. Stravinsky's work extended over several years, and the ballet, initially entitled *Les Noces Villageoises*, was staged ten years after the score had been commissioned.

On November 1, 1914, Diaghilev wrote to Stravinsky: "At what stage are you with *Noces*?" On March 3, 1915, he alerted Stravinsky that he would be arriving for the score: "Expect us [Diaghilev and Massine] around March 12. See that you have a great ballet ready."

But in January of 1922 Stravinsky was still writing, this time to me: "So, around the first of February, or mid-month, the whole opera [*Mavra*] will be finished. Then I'll tackle the scoring of *Noces*."

The first exchanges of ideas between Diaghilev and Stravinsky on the subject of *Les Noces* dated back to a period when Nijinsky, in his capacity as choreographer for the company, took part in their conversations. But in November, 1914, after he had broken with Nijinsky, Diaghilev wrote to Stravinsky:

The invention of the movement for Noces *is clearly Nijinsky's, but I don't want to discuss*

Sketch for *Les Noces*, by Nathalie Gontcharova

the matter with him for several months. As for Massine, he is still too young, but every day he grows to be more one of us, and that's the important thing.

While Stravinsky was working on the score, Gontcharova designed in succession three different versions of sets and costumes for *Les Noces.*

The first two—one in folkloristic, peasant style, with brilliant colors, and the other worked out in half-tones which were overembellished with gold and silver embroidery—Diaghilev rejected.

For the third and final version, Diaghilev asked Gontcharova to design the costumes after the cut of the regulation work clothes that the company dancers wore during rehearsals —short trousers and shirts for the men, tunics for the women. It was easy to "Russianize" these costumes by lengthening the women's tunics to convert them into *sarafans* (an old style of Russian peasant dress) and by changing the neckline of the men's shirts to turn them into villagers. Diaghilev established just two models—one for men and one for women—for all the performers in *Les Noces,* and he limited the colors to brown and white.

Although Massine was originally to have created the choreography, by 1923, when Diaghilev decided to produce the ballet, he was no longer a member of the Ballets Russes, and Diaghilev was obliged to consider the collaboration of another choreographer.

Bronislava Nijinska had been the official choreographer of the company since 1921, yet Diaghilev hesitated a long time before entrusting her with the creation of *Les Noces.* He was concerned that the task might be too demanding for her, and he was skeptical about her being sufficiently imaginative. However, their very first conversation about the ballet reassured him, and any mistrust evaporated when he heard Nijinska say, "*Noces* is a ballet that must be danced on point. That will elongate the dancers' silhouettes and make them resemble the saints in Byzantine mosaics."

Sketch for
Les Noces, by
Nathalie Gontcharova

Ensemble,
scene from *Les Noces,*
1923

Contrary to his custom, after Nijinska had made this observation Diaghilev never interfered in her work, and he came to her rehearsals only to approve unreservedly her choreographing of *Les Noces*.

However, the formula of a "ballet on point" as applied by Nijinska in this work threw the company's dancers into great confusion. For them, "point" was synonymous with the classical choreography of Petipa and meant variations on *The Sleeping Beauty*. Yet now, Felia Doubrovska, for example, who had eagerly accepted the role of the Bride, found herself condemned to remain motionless or to mark time *on point*.

In Paris, *Les Noces* was a triumphant success, but in London, three years later, the ballet was coolly received. Among the few English admirers of the work was H. G. Wells, who went on record with a statement published in June, 1923:

Stravinsky

Ensemble, scenes from *Les Noces*, 1923

I have been very much astonished at the reception of "Les Noces" by several of the leading London critics. There seems to be some undercurrent of artistic politics in the business. I find in several of the criticisms to which I object, sneers at the "élite," and in one of them a puff of some competing show. Writing as an old-fashioned popular writer, not at all of the highbrow sect, I feel bound to bear my witness on the other side. I do not know of any other ballet so interesting, so amusing, so fresh or nearly so exciting as "Les Noces." I want to see it again and again, and because I want to do so I protest against this conspiracy of wilful stupidity that may succeed in driving it out of the programme.

How wilful the stupidity is, the efforts of one of our professional guides of taste to consider the four grand pianos on the stage as part of the scene, bear witness.

Another of these guardians of culture treats the amusing plainness of the backcloth, with its single window to indicate one house and its two windows for the other, as imaginative poverty—even he could have thought of a stove and a table;—and they all cling to the suggestion that Stravinsky has tried to make marriage "attractive" and failed in the attempt. Of course they make jokes about the mother-in-law; that was unavoidable. It will be an extraordinary loss to the London public if this deliberate dullness of its advisers robs it of "Les Noces."

That ballet is a rendering in sound and vision of the peasant soul, in its gravity, in its deliberate and simple-minded intricacy, in its subtly varied rhythms, in its deep undercurrents of excitement, that will astonish and delight every intelligent man or woman who goes to see it. The silly pretty-pretty tradition of Watteau and Fragonard is flung aside. Instead of fancy dress peasants we have peasants in plain black and white, and the smirking flirtatiousness of Daphnis and Chloë gives place to a richly humorous solemnity. It was an amazing experience to come out from this delightful display with the warp and woof of music and vision still running and interweaving in one's mind, and find a little group of critics flushed with resentment and ransacking the stores of their minds for cheap trite depreciation of the freshest, and strongest thing that they had had a chance to praise for a long time.

H. G. Wells

192

Picasso drawings for
the illustrated programs of the
1923 Ballets Russes season

A PICASSO
IMPROMPTU

In 1923, Diaghilev made me responsible for the artistic supervision of the illustrated programs of the Ballets Russes. I wanted to publish some Picasso drawings in the program for the Monte Carlo season, and asked him to let me have some of the studies of dancers which he had made during rehearsals in Rome, in 1917. Picasso promised he would find them somewhere in his studio, and so that he might think of them in relation to a layout, I took him, as a kind of dummy, several sheets of drawing paper trimmed to indicate the program's format.

Picasso gave me a date when I could come for the sketches, but when I arrived, I found that he had not had time to look for them; he would give them to me another time. Over a period of weeks, I kept going back, spent hours with him in friendly talk, but always left empty-handed. Sometimes he would take me into his studio to show me his most recent canvases and let me see for myself the indescribable litter in this room where, somewhere, the drawings I was waiting for lay buried.

The printer was growing impatient, however, and he tried to persuade me to give up the idea of publishing the Picasso drawings. Finally, he gave me one last deadline for their delivery, but that day Picasso had still not found them. I resigned myself to leaving with nothing but the now useless dummy.

As I got up to go, Picasso seemed to be struck by an idea. He grew animated, as if he had just realized that since it was a matter of drawings he himself had done, he could remedy the situation with no trouble, without even having to get up.

He took a stub of pencil from his pocket and, in a few minutes, covered the pages of the dummy with admirable drawings of dancers.

Cover of Ballets Russes program, by Picasso

Auric, Cocteau, and Poulenc, Monte Carlo, 1924

LES TENTATIONS
DE LA
BERGERE
OU
L'AMOUR VAINQUEUR

Ballet in one act. Music by Michel de Montéclair (1666–1737), reconstructed and scored by Henri Casadesus. Choreography by Bronislava Nijinska. Curtain, décor, and costumes by Juan Gris. First performance: Casino, Monte Carlo, January 3, 1924.

In the autumn of 1922, when Diaghilev signed his first long-term (six-month) contract with the Société des Bains de Mer de Monaco, he had plans for a French festival, to be given at the Monte Carlo Casino. There was a delay, however, before the project could be realized, and the festival did not take place until January, 1924.

As the core of the dance section of the festival, Diaghilev chose the ballets he had already commissioned from Francis Poulenc and Georges Auric—*Les Biches* and *Les Fâcheux*—and led off the operatic offerings with Gounod's opéra comique *Philémon et Baucis*, which he had "discovered" when he heard it at a Sunday matinee at the Théâtre du Trianon Lyrique.

The staging of *Philémon et Baucis* had been lamentable, but Diaghilev was enthusiastic about the Gounod score and soon after, on August 8, 1922, he wrote me from Lyons, where he had gone to find singers for the festival: "On leaving the station, I went to a matinee of *Gianni Schicchi* and in the evening heard a work of genius called *Faust*."

Accordingly, Diaghilev decided to make the works of Gounod the basis of the operatic portion of the festival, and he had started looking for an early musical score to round out the program of ballets.

With the help of Henri Casadesus, he collected some fragments of compositions by Michel de Montéclair, which were in the library of the Paris Opéra, and these he adapted to the story line of the dance interlude in Tchaikovsky's *Queen of Spades*. The original title

A Boris Kochno
Bien cordialement
Juan Gris

BORIS

of the interlude—"The Sincerity of a Shepherdess"—was changed by Diaghilev to "The Temptations of a Shepherdess." For the mise-en-scène, he approached Juan Gris.

Gris's first contacts with the Ballets Russes went back to the spring of 1921, when, at Diaghilev's request, he had come to Monte Carlo to paint the portraits of Slavinsky and Larionov, who were creating the choreography for *Chout*. After Gris completed this commission, which Diaghilev had offered him with an eye to the illustrated program for the forthcoming Paris season, he painted portraits of me and of Maria Dalbaicin.

Actually, this commission was Diaghilev's way of compensating Gris for the fact that the *Cuadro Flamenco* sets, which had been destined for him, had in the end been done by Picasso. And although in 1921 Gris had submitted to Diaghilev another ballet project for which he had written the book and designed the sets, he did not take part in a Ballets Russes production until 1923.

This first collaboration between Diaghilev and Gris involved a gala given at Versailles on June 30 of that year. The spectacle, entitled "*La Fête Merveilleuse*," was organized by Diaghilev at the request of Gabriel Astruc. It took place in the Hall of Mirrors in the Château, and was followed by a candlelight supper in the Hall of Battles and by a display of light effects and fireworks in the park.

For this soirée, Gris conceived the decoration of the stage which had been constructed in the Hall of Mirrors for the evening's entertainment, and he designed the costumes for the singer, Maria Kuznetsova, and for two heralds, the dancer Singayevsky and me. Attired as a Roman warrior (after seventeenth-century paintings) and accompanied by the blaring of trumpets, I strode onto the platform to announce the beginning of the entertainment. It was to be my one appearance in a theatrical performance.

Later, for the French festival in Monte Carlo, Diaghilev commissioned Gris to design the sets for two operas, *La Colombe* by Gounod and *L'Éducation Manquée* by Chabrier.

Sketch by Juan Gris for *Les Tentations de la Bergère,* with a dedication to Diaghilev, 1922

LE
MEDECIN
MALGRE LUI

Opéra comique in three acts by Jules Barbier and Michel Carré, after the comedy by Molière. Music by Charles Gounod. Recitatifs by Erik Satie. Sets and costumes by Alexandre Benois. First performance: Casino, Monte Carlo, January 5, 1924.

In 1923, Diaghilev commissioned Alexandre Benois to design the mise-en-scène for Gounod's opera *Le Médecin Malgré Lui*, which was to be included in the repertoire for the January, 1924, opera season in Monte Carlo.

The last time Benois had taken part in a Diaghilev production had been in 1914, when he designed the scenery and costumes for Stravinsky's *Le Chant du Rossignol*. In reply to Diaghilev's letter offering him the commission for *Le Médecin Malgré Lui*, Benois wrote from Petrograd.

Dear friend Seryozha!

After a nine-year interval, I am renewing relations with you which will, I hope, be lasting, and will, perhaps, continue indefinitely. To my regret, I am not familiar with this opera by Gounod, but am counting on Asafiev to obtain the piano score for me. However, since I have enormous regard for this "forgotten" musician, I am persuaded in advance that the work is beautiful and beguiling. In any event, I am delighted that we shall be working together again in an atmosphere that I consider—as I used to—family-like. And lastly, in an opera that owes its origin to my beloved Molière I will very likely find a great deal of "stimulating" material.

I shall probably not manage to leave here before the end of July. That is not too late, I hope? Then we should count on two or three weeks for the journey and for me to recover my wits. I simply must take a rather long bath of social hygiene so as to become again what I once was—what, for that matter, I have never stopped being in my essential substance. (Not badly put!) So, according to my calculations, I could start work around August 20. . . .

Who will build the sets? Please, may it be Allegri! Ah, yes, my Coca [Nicholas, Benois's son] would also be available. A fine master painter he's turned out to be, the young puppy.

Benois ended his letter:

And so, my dear, I should like to think that in the very near future I shall be embracing your fresh and voluminous self, shall see again the famous gray streak which, I hope, still stands out against the blackness of your hair, rediscover your toothy smile and, what is most important, receive from you a jolt of that superb force of will which has always had so beneficial an effect on me. I'm going to try, in my turn, to be at my best!

Benois reached Monte Carlo in the autumn of 1923, and his mise-en-scène for the opera was completed well before the opening of Diaghilev's opera season, which was preceded by a theatrical season organized by René Blum.

The Molière play was to be part of the program for the theatrical season also, and Blum had asked Diaghilev to lend him the costumes Benois had designed for the Gounod opera. Diaghilev authorized their use, but he was away from Monte Carlo and could give Blum no indication of which costumes were for whom. They reached Blum all jumbled together in baskets, and he distributed them to his company at random, having no notion for which character Benois had intended what.

Diaghilev did not return to Monte Carlo until the day of Blum's dress rehearsal. As he walked into the theatre, he saw a woman onstage whom he took to be a walk-on, for the costume she was wearing had been intended for one of the members of the corps de ballet. It had, however, been entirely altered to the actress's taste.

Outraged by this "butchery," Diaghilev interrupted the rehearsal, shouting, "Who is this mouse? . . . Remove her. . . . Get her offstage and get that costume off her! She's completely ruined it!"

Blum came rushing up to explain that the "mouse" was the celebrated actress Alice Cocéa, who was playing the lead in the Molière play and whom he had mistakenly fitted out in a corps de ballet costume.

LES BICHES

Ballet with songs, in one act. Music by Francis Poulenc. Choreography by Bronislava Nijinska. Curtain, décor, and costumes by Marie Laurencin. First performance: Casino, Monte Carlo, January 6, 1924.

In May, 1921, Diaghilev heard the music Poulenc had composed for a play by Radiguet and Cocteau, *Le Gendarme Incompris,* which Pierre Bertin was then presenting at the Théâtre Michel. This music prompted Diaghilev to commission Poulenc to write a ballet score for him.

At the time, Poulenc had already begun composing a ballet score to a scenario by Mme. Bongard, which was to be called *Les Demoiselles.* In the course of his work for Diaghilev, however, the early title and even the scenario of this ballet were discarded. In the end, Poulenc's work became a suite of dances with no real plot, and it was entitled *Les Biches.*

On September 24, 1922, Poulenc wrote to Diaghilev from Nazelle, Indre-et-Loire:

My dear Diaghilev:

How difficult it is to get in touch with you! I have written you in Deauville and at the Continental, but all in vain; both letters have been returned to me. May I finally, through the

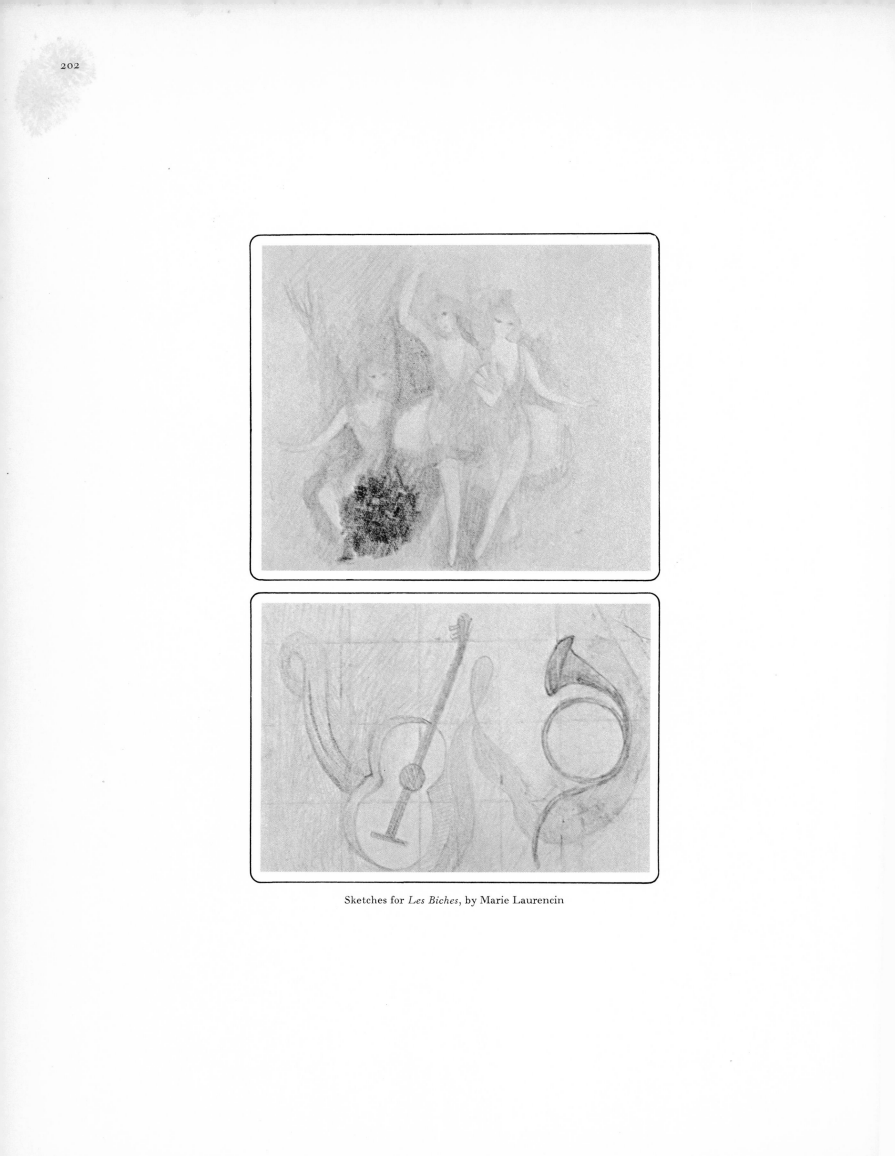

Sketches for *Les Biches*, by Marie Laurencin

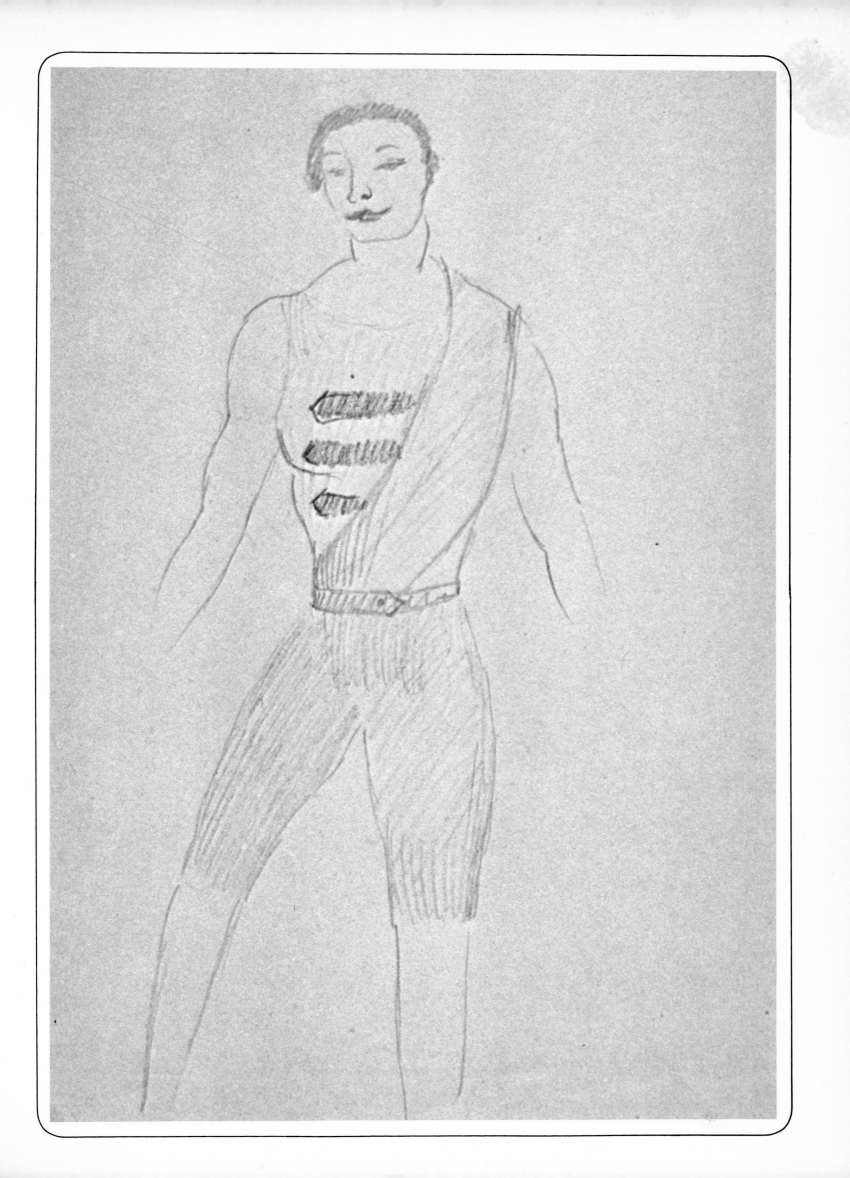

good offices of dear Stravinsky, let you know that the name for the ballet has been found—Les Biches. Up to now, the new title has garnered all votes, and I hope it will have yours. It is so Marie Laurencin.

I shall be staying on here until December 20, working for you. I think you will be pleased with me. I've finished the introduction, which runs two minutes fifteen seconds, also the presto (No. 1); the song for the three men becomes No. 2. I've put it there because as No. 7 it would not have provided enough contrast, being in the same spirit as the final number (8). So now the drawling song of the three women will be 7.

I have finally found my No. 3 (a star's solo), but how hard it was. I hope now that I've avoided the 1830 waltz, the 1870 waltz, the Italian adagio, the Casella "false-notes waltz," and the sad waltz (Parade). Actually, it's a very supple number in 2/4 time, very danceable and andantino; it begins in C flat, then slips into the most unexpected modulations. I am sure it's just what is needed.

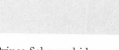

Prince Schervashidze,
by Pruna

————

Bronislava Nijinska
in *Les Biches*

I'm at the beginning of the game (No. 4) now; in the first measures, the singers count "ams, tram, dram, pic et pic et colédram," etc. . . . then the dancers divide into two camps and the game begins. A kind of hunting game, very Louis Quatorze. The mazurka-rag (No. 5) is scary. Tell Nijinska that from now on she can think in terms of frenetic movements in three tempi. Still to be done is No. 6 (a pas de deux), for which I have, alas, not the glimmer of an idea; also the song for No. 7 and the final rondeau, for which I do have a few ideas.

I'm estimating my orchestra (by threes) for a hall on the Châtelet-Mogador scale. So I hope we won't have to move on to the Opéra. It's the same with Auric's orchestra. What do you think of all this?

Write me soon. Greetings to you and to Boris.

Francis Poulenc

When Diaghilev was back in Paris, he got together frequently with Poulenc, who would play him bits from the ballet he was composing. They met at the Hôtel Meurice, in the apartment of Misia Sert, to whom Poulenc dedicated the score of *Les Biches*.

Poulenc was a brilliant pianist, but his attitude baffled Diaghilev, for when he asked him to repeat a piece he had just played, Poulenc used to improvise, saying that his final version would be "on the same order."

Sometimes Poulenc would break off playing and ask Diaghilev anxiously, "Doesn't that sound like *Mavra*?" When this was repeated to Stravinsky, he laughed and said, "In some cases, it's better to imitate good music than to write one's own."

Although to Poulenc Diaghilev praised Nijinska to the heavens, he was much concerned when he entrusted the choreography of *Les Biches* to her, for until then she had choreographed for his company only the eminently Russian works of Stravinsky, and Diaghilev feared she might be unresponsive to the Latin charm of the Poulenc score. His concern seemed justified by the news he was receiving from Monaco, where, in his absence, Nijinska was creating the dances for *Les Biches*. In fact, people who saw the early rehearsals spoke of a great similarity between the choreography of the new ballet and that of *Les Noces*. However, after Diaghilev had returned to Monte Carlo, he wrote me:

Nemtchinova
and Vilzak
in *Les Biches*

———

Nemtchinova

> *1923*
>
> *Hôtel de Paris*
>
> *Monte Carlo*
>
> *Here everything is going along much better than I had expected. Poulenc is enthusiastic about Bronya's [Nijinska's] choreography, and they get along excellently together. The choreography has delighted and astonished me. But then, this good woman, intemperate and antisocial as she is, does belong to the Nijinsky family.*
>
> *Here and there her choreography is perhaps a bit too ordinary, a bit too* feminine, *but,* on the whole, *it is very good. The dance for the three men has come out extremely well, and they perform it with bravura—weightily, like three cannon. It doesn't at all resemble* Noces, *any more than Tchaikovsky's* Eugene Onegin *resembles his* Queen of Spades.
>
> *All the girls in the corps de ballet are mad about Poulenc. They go about humming his music, and say that he's an accomplished flirt.*
>
> *This is the picture. Tomorrow is a holiday, and all Monte Carlo is hung with splendid flags.*

At the same time, I received a letter from Poulenc, in which he wrote:

> *I'm eager to show you my orchestra and Nijinska's choreography, which is* truly *splendid. The pas de deux is so beautiful that all the dancers insist on watching it. I am enchanted.*

Diaghilev had returned to Paris from Monte Carlo when he received the following letter from Poulenc:

> *Friday Evening*
>
> *Excellency:*
>
> *You cannot imagine what you have missed for the last two days. When Nemtchinova's dance is finished—and what a* miracle*—they start the game. I must say that as* madness *it surpasses anything one could imagine. Nijinska is really a* genius. *Listen to this: having decided that the sofa is a "star," just as she herself is, she is making it dance throughout the game!!! Grigoriev asked the Casino for the loan of a magnificent sofa, and they fell to work (in an entirely proper fashion, naturally).*

*I shan't try to describe to you what happens. In a "presto" movement, the women take sitting positions, leap into the air, fall onto the tufted cushions, roll over on their backs (although the two men are straddling the sofa back), and then they drag the poor sofa, which must be ultrasolid, in all directions. When, in the middle section, the music calms down, the Star and Vilzak bounce onstage. Thereupon the Girls turn the sofa (its back is now to the audience) into an observatory, their heads popping up over the back and then dropping out of sight; when the game resumes—*now listen to this—*the two men quickly turn the sofa around and there are the two women lying down in a position that, thinking of Barbette, I can only describe as head to tail.*

Nijinska, 1923

You see, this is not at all bad. As to the last detail, I think it's the same sort of thing as the horse on Marie's curtain, and that it's myopia rather than sadism on Nijinska's part. Be that as it may, our two ladies complement each other very well indeed.

This is all the news I have for you. It's good news, you must admit. At rehearsals, I laugh until I cry. It seems to me, furthermore, that from the public's point of view, all this will be irresistible.

Come back soon. A thousand greetings to dear Boris, whom I miss, and to you, "Milord."

Poulenc

The collaboration of Marie Laurencin was a fresh source of worry for Diaghilev. When it came to sketches for the mise-en-scène, she delivered to the wardrobe mistress, Vera Soudeikine, and to the scene-painter, Prince Schervashidze, designs and water colors that were charming but so completely lacking in precise detail that they could not be used as models to work from.

Dissatisfied with the results produced by the staff, Laurencin would intervene to correct their work, and often, after several unsuccessful versions, she would make them restore what she had made them change. When she saw the set that Schervashidze had executed in scrupulous accord with her design, Laurencin had him change it, but then, disappointed in the outcome, she went back to the original version.

When Mme. Soudeikine shipped the costumes from Paris, she warned Diaghilev that they bore no relation to the sketches he had approved because when they were being made, Laurencin, accompanied by Misia Sert, had constantly come to supervise the work and had completely altered them.

For example, the costume for the principal dancer, Vera Nemtchinova, which was designed as a dress with a long train, became, after Laurencin's revisions, a simple jerkin— so simple that it caused the Monte Carlo authorities to intervene. René Léon, director of the Société des Bains de Mer de Monaco, informed Diaghilev that some prudish shareholders in the Société were scandalized by Nemtchinova's costume; they considered it indecent and wanted a skirt or classic tutu to be added.

PHILEMON
ET BAUCIS

Opera in two acts by Jules Barbier and Michel Carré. Music by Charles Gounod. Décor and costumes by Alexandre Benois. First performance: Casino, Monte Carlo, January 10, 1924.

Diaghilev admired immensely Picasso's paintings of mythological scenes, and asked him to design the sets and costumes for Gounod's opera *Philémon et Baucis*.

Picasso declined the commission, but every time the two men met, he would question Diaghilev about the opera, which led Diaghilev to hope that his refusal was not final. He arranged to have the score played for Picasso, thinking that this might persuade him to accept. Picasso listened to the music, glum and scowling; he came to life only to make various comments that disconcerted Diaghilev. For example, he suggested that a chorus of music-hall girls come onstage to the music intended for a procession of bacchantes, and, in the heat of the discussion, he performed a French cancan number himself.

As difficult and disappointing as Diaghilev found this interview, he persevered and finally won Picasso's promise to collaborate on *Philémon et Baucis*. Delighted with his victory, Diaghilev took off for Monte Carlo, leaving me in Paris with instructions to urge on Picasso's labors.

On the appointed day, I went to Picasso's house for the designs. He led me into his studio and over to a children's theatre. Raising the curtain, he disclosed a composition of bits of wood, sacking, and string that was a far cry from the Hellenic décor Diaghilev was dreaming of.

Picasso had not yet begun work on the sketches for the costumes, but he asked me to write Diaghilev that he wanted all the dancers to wear all-white rehearsal tights. "About the color of the paper on which I'm going to sketch them," he added.

Without going back to Picasso, Diaghilev ordered the mise-en-scène from Alexandre Benois.

Recalling these details about *Philémon et Baucis* takes me back to Picasso's apartment, at 23 rue de la Boétie, where, in 1923, we used to meet almost daily.

As one entered the vestibule, one saw two very large paintings by Le Douanier Rousseau, one an allegory based on Bastille Day and the other a canvas known as "Portrait of Yadviga."

Picasso told me one day that he had come across this portrait in a secondhand shop, behind a stack of canvases that concealed three-quarters of the Rousseau painting. The head of the portrait extended above the other canvases and, in the gloom of the shop, looked to Picasso as if it were a small canvas resting on top of the others. The shopkeeper asked a hundred sous for it and, wanting to take his purchase with him, Picasso pulled out from the pile of paintings the enormous "Portrait of Yadviga."

Other works by early or contemporary artists appeared on the walls of Picasso's apartment from time to time, but Diaghilev never seemed to notice them. Here, on rue de la Boétie, he gave the impression of wearing blinders, which he removed only in front of Picasso's work.

When he was received by Picasso and his wife, Olga, Diaghilev would wait impatiently for Picasso to take his studio keys from his pocket, and he would enter the atelier with respect and obvious emotion. Diaghilev never said to Picasso, as he used to say to Cocteau, "Astonish me!" But whenever he went to see Picasso, he looked like someone who knows he is on the road to important discoveries.

Picasso never showed his paintings except in the room that served as his studio. Indeed, he never took them out of the studio after the day he had hung a huge Harlequin, done in pastels, on the drawing-room wall and had come back an hour later to find his work completely erased. A new and overzealous servant had "cleaned" the canvas with a wet cloth.

During those 1923 visits, Picasso talked constantly to Diaghilev about a project for a ballet to be called *La Petite Fille Écrasée*. Picasso was to be the sole creator of the scenario, music, choreography, and mise-en-scène for this ballet, of which nothing has ever existed except the title.

Another of Picasso's ideas was a ballet in which the dancers would be dressed as flies and would move against a gigantic still life of a butcher shop.

LES FÂCHEUX

Ballet in one act by Boris Kochno, after the comedy-ballet by Molière. Music by Georges Auric. Choreography by Bronislava Nijinska. Curtain, décor, and costumes by Georges Braque. First performance: Casino, Monte Carlo, January 19, 1924.

In the spring of 1922, in anticipation of the French festival at Monte Carlo, Diaghilev asked Georges Auric to write the score for *Les Fâcheux*. For this ballet, Auric agreed to rework and expand the incidental music he had previously composed for Pierre Bertin's production of the Molière comedy at the Théâtre de l'Odéon. Diaghilev entrusted me with the task of dividing the action of the play into dance sequences, preserving, however, the thread of Molière's amorous intrigue.

The production of *Les Fâcheux* was accompanied by numerous misadventures, the first of which was precipitated by Braque's curtain.

Set for *Les Fâcheux*, by Braque

In working on his sketches, Braque followed the Molière text scrupulously. He began with the design of a drop curtain for the prologue, although the prologue was not to have been included in the ballet. Diaghilev was so enthusiastic about Braque's drawing, which represented a naked nymph against a background of greenery, that he decided to add a prologue, using Auric's overture. But the dancers Diaghilev selected for the nymph refused, one after another, to appear onstage in a costume they considered indecent.

After the first performance, in which the role was danced by L. Krassovska, Braque substituted for a live dancer a nymph that he himself painted in the center of the curtain.

The costume for Lysander provoked another incident.

The incidental role of the ballet master in *Les Fâcheux* had originally been intended for one of the premiers danseurs of the company, Stanislas Idzikowski, who accepted it against his will. When the costumes, which had been executed in Paris under Braque's direction, were delivered to the theatre in Monte Carlo, Lysander's was not entirely dry, because Braque had had it dyed and then washed several times in an effort to achieve the exact tint of his drawing. During dress rehearsal, the costume left some traces of dye on Idzikowski's skin, which he made the pretext for refusing to appear in what was a secondary role, and on the night of the première he was replaced by Nijinska.

When the time came to construct the set for *Les Fâcheux*, Braque, who had come down to Monte Carlo, supervised closely the progress of the work, and he rarely left the workshop

Auric, Braque, and Boris Kochno, Monte Carlo, 1924

Costume designs for *Les Fâcheux*, by Braque

where Prince Schervashidze and his assistants were building the scenery. During the hours when the crew of painters knocked off work, Braque would sometimes join Diaghilev and me in the exotic gardens of the Casino, but he always seemed worried that he would be late for the resumption of the work. Seated on a bench in the shade of the palm trees or at a table on the terrace of the Café de Paris—always wearing a bowler hat—he would tell stories of his youth and hum, "*Je cherche après Titine, Titine, ma Titine,*" but his eyes never strayed from the Casino clock, and when he left us, he headed straight for the workshop. In overseeing the execution of the ballet costumes, Braque scrupulously, constantly consulted his sketches. A letter I received from him the evening before the Paris première of *Les Fâcheux* indicates what importance he attached to the smallest detail of his mise-en-scène. He was writing about an infinitesimal touch of red in the costumes for the corps de ballet:

My dear Kochno:

Set my mind at rest. Tell me whether the red on the masks has been replaced. Diaghilev promised me this would be done. (A brown, for example, like the back of Orphise, would do well and the combination would be perfect.) Take care of this, please. Best to you.

G. Braque

Massine
in *Les Fâcheux*
———
Tchernicheva
and Massine
in *Les Fâcheux*

The back of the women's costumes in *Les Fâcheux* was different from the front. The front, vertically divided in half, into a right and a left side, had been copied from engravings of ladies' fashions of the seventeenth and eighteenth centuries, while the back was a uniform brown.

Braque's idea was to make the dancers disappear completely from the audience's view without their having to leave the stage; they could simply turn their backs to the audience and thus blend in with the scenery. Unhappily, Nijinska had not kept Braque's intentions in mind, and she devised a conventional pantomime on the theme of Molière's comedy.

The first version of Auric's score included an important "Nocturne" that Diaghilev eliminated from the ballet. Later, Nijinska created a variation to this music for Dolin, who performed it on point.

In 1927, in Monte Carlo, Massine created a new choreographic version of *Les Fâcheux*, using Braque's mise-en-scène.

As for Georges Auric, my only recollections of his visit to Monte Carlo in 1923 are of his disappearing frequently into the gambling rooms of the Casino during rehearsals of his ballet, and his inviting me to succulent luncheons à deux on the terrace of the restaurant of Monsieur Ré.

LE TRAIN BLEU

Choreographed operetta, in one act. Libretto by Jean Cocteau. Music by Darius Milhaud. Choreography by Bronislava Nijinska. Décor by Henri Laurens. Curtain by Pablo Picasso. Costumes by Gabrielle Chanel. First performance: Théâtre des Champs-Élysées, Paris, June 13, 1924.

On the title page of Milhaud's first manuscript there appears, in Cocteau's handwriting:

à Serge Diaghilev

"Le Train Bleu"

Opérette dansée, 1924.

Collaborateurs: Mmes G. Chanel, Nijinska.

MM. Jean Cocteau, Laurens, Darius Milhaud.

Darius Milhaud and Diaghilev, London, 1924

Patrick Kay, otherwise known as Anton Dolin, had been engaged to dance in the Diaghilev company's corps de ballet early in the London rehearsals of *The Sleeping Beauty* at the Alhambra, in 1921. Under the pseudonym of Patrikeyev, he took part in the ensemble scenes and danced a pas de huit in the Prologue, which Diaghilev called "the little waltz." (One day Stravinsky told me that he had dreamed he composed the music for this waltz.)

At the end of the Alhambra engagement, Patrick Kay remained in London and continued to study at the school identified on its letterhead as the "Russian Dancing Academy Organised by Princess Seraphina Astafieva," which was directed by a dancer formerly with the Maryinsky and later with the Ballets Russes.

In June, 1923, Astafieva wrote Diaghilev recommending one of her young pupils and proposed bringing him to Paris for an audition. Astafieva's protégé was Patrick Kay—Patrikeyev. On the strength of this audition, he was engaged by Diaghilev and, in January, 1924, in Monte Carlo, under the name of Anton Dolin he danced the principal role in the revival of *Daphnis et Chloë*.

(For this revival, Diaghilev had Bakst's décor and costumes restored, and commissioned Juan Gris to design a new Daphnis costume for Dolin.)

In other ballets then in the repertoire, Dolin danced less important roles and, during the Ballets Russes season of April, 1924, in Barcelona, Diaghilev wrote me:

What truly *delights me is Patrick's dancing. He dances in a* truly *adorable way. In* Carnaval, Cimarosiana, *and* Pulcinella, *he is almost better than the other dancers. Perhaps this impression is due only to the novelty of his appearance, but he does possess a true style, and that is important.*

Immediately after Dolin's debut in *Daphnis et Chloë*, Diaghilev, wanting to emphasize the acrobatic capacities of the young dancer, asked Jean Cocteau, who happened to be in Monte Carlo at the time, for the scenario of a new ballet.

Diaghilev was enthusiastic about the development of contemporary French operetta and the music of Christine and Maurice Yvain, so he suggested that Cocteau concoct the plot for a choreographed musical comedy. Cocteau wrote a scenario for a "choreographed operetta," which he first entitled *Le Beau Gosse*, then *Les Poules*, and, finally, *Le Train Bleu*. This last was taken from the name of the fastest and most luxurious train of the day, which was on the Paris–Côte d'Azur run.

Diaghilev knew that Darius Milhaud was highly adaptable; the composer had proved as much in 1923, when he composed the music for the recitatifs in Chabrier's comic opera *L'Éducation Manquée* for the Monte Carlo opera season. Therefore, Diaghilev commissioned Milhaud to write the score for *Le Train Bleu*, which was completed between February 15 and March 5, 1924. In his *Notes sans Musique*, Milhaud relates his recollections of this ballet:

Anton Dolin
in *Pulcinella*,
1924

Dolin,
costumed for
*Les Tentations de
la Bergère*,
and Henri Laurens

Le Train Bleu was an operetta without words. When Diaghilev asked me to do the music for Cocteau's scenario, which was light and frivolous and gay, in the manner of Offenbach, he knew quite well that I would not be able to go in for my usual kind of music, which he did not like. The action takes place in a fashionable vacation spot where the elegant train, "Le Bleu," disgorges new bathers daily; they exercise on the stage and practice their favorite sports —tennis, golf, etc. Dolin could give himself up to his acrobatics and choreographic fantasies. Throughout the rehearsals, Messager [André Messager was directing the orchestra] was paternal, charming, and full of interested concern. The performances were without incident.

Nevertheless, the preparation of this production was rife with complications arising from the different ideas of Cocteau and Nijinska, who was then the official choreographer of the Ballets Russes.

Cocteau was used to taking an active part in the staging of his works for the theatre, and he had given Nijinska numerous suggestions for the choreography, which she was to create in his absence. The manuscript of the scenario which he had prepared for Nijinska's use was filled with examples she was to follow in developing the ballet. As models, he cited a pair of acrobatic dancers who, that year, were appearing at Ciro's late in the evening, snapshots of the Prince of Wales playing golf, slow-motion films of foot races, and so forth.

The personalities and events from which Cocteau proposed that Nijinska draw her inspiration belonged to the worldly milieu of the day—a milieu that Nijinska, who led a quiet, secluded life, didn't know and, furthermore, detested. She did not speak French and so could not explain herself to Cocteau or get him to accept her ideas. Although Diaghilev used to intervene, acting as interpreter and mediator, their relations from the outset were tense, if not hostile.

Cocteau was disappointed by Nijinska's attitude and, after returning to Paris, he wrote to Diaghilev on February 29:

Darius is in good form. He has recopied the fourteen minutes, and is working ahead. The best thing would be for me to wait for you and go back with you. Ask Nijinska how she's feeling about me. I am not going to make a move unless I am sure she will listen to me, for ridiculous diplomatic games are useless. I do not insist that my name appear on the program as director (although my researches in relation to details of the staging have a logical place in my work), but, in exchange, I do insist on being listened to.

However, after Cocteau's departure from Monte Carlo, Diaghilev had reasoned with Nijinska, who seemed to accept his directives, and when she began in April, in Barcelona, to choreograph the ballet, I received a letter from Diaghilev saying:

Bronya [Nijinska] is staging Le Train Bleu, *and I very much like the first dance, which is quite gymnastic. I made a long speech to the company, explaining just what the word*

"operetta" means, what Milhaud's music is about, and what is, in my view, the plastic problem that this ballet presents. I was listened to with devout attention. I think everything will be all right and hope that, minus Harlequins and Colombines, this ballet will be a true expression of ourselves.

By the time the company reached Paris, the choreography for *Le Train Bleu* was still incomplete, but the sections Nijinska had created were enough to aggravate the hostility between her and Cocteau.

Declaring that Nijinska had not followed his directions, Cocteau persuaded her to modify the numbers she had done. When she came to putting the finishing touches on a new version of the ballet, he intervened again and, in highhanded fashion, interrupted rehearsals, and substituted pantomime scenes for dances that Nijinska had created.

The atmosphere at rehearsals was highly charged, and, on the verge of the opening, the dancers still did not know whether they should obey Cocteau or Nijinska.

The dress rehearsal of *Le Train Bleu* took place the same day as the première but before the heat in the theatre had been turned on. The dancers came onstage in Chanel's bathing suits, which they had not tried on before, and the sight of those bathers shivering on the beach in costumes that did not fit them was both lamentable and laughable.

When the curtain rose on this dismaying spectacle, Diaghilev fled to the last row of the balcony. He felt utterly powerless to remedy the disaster, and asked me which of the other ballets could be substituted for *Le Train Bleu* at this last moment.

After the rehearsal that day, not one member of the company left the theatre. The few hours that remained before the performance enabled Nijinska to revise her choreography, the dancers to learn their new steps, and the wardrobe women to adjust the costumes.

By evening the ballet was so altered as to be unrecognizable and, thanks largely to Dolin's acrobatic prowess, was a great success.

In the spring of 1924, during one of our visits to Picasso in Paris, Diaghilev had admired in his studio a painting of two women running along a beach, and he had asked Picasso's permission to use it as a model for the *Train Bleu* curtain.

The execution of the curtain Diaghilev entrusted to Prince Schervashidze, and when the work was finished, Picasso came to the Théâtre des Champs-Élysées one morning, found absolutely nothing to retouch, and wrote at the bottom of the curtain: "Dedicated to Diaghilev. Picasso 24."

For the presentation of the Picasso curtain, Diaghilev commissioned Auric to compose a "Fanfare."

The following year, Picasso was vacationing in Monte Carlo with his wife, Olga, and his son, Paul. He knew that Diaghilev and I were building a library of Russian books, and he said to me, "One day I'll design for you a bookplate that will be a quatrain in a universal language, for the forms of objects rhyme as words do. In painting, melon rhymes with mandolin."

Scenes
from *Le Train Bleu*

Dolin in
Le Train Bleu

Enrico Cecchetti
by Picasso,
Monte Carlo, 1925

Max Reinhardt,
Morris Gest, Diaghilev,
and Otto Kahn,
Lido, August, 1926

ZEPHYR ET FLORE

Ballet in three scenes by Boris Kochno. Music by Vladimir Dukelsky. Choreography by Leonide Massine. Décor and costumes by Georges Braque. First performance: Casino, Monte Carlo, April 28, 1925. First performance in Paris: Théâtre de la Gaîté-Lyrique, June 15, 1925. First performance of revised version by Braque: Théâtre Sarah Bernhardt, May 27, 1926.

In 1924, Diaghilev learned that a young Russian composer, Vladimir Dukelsky, who had emigrated to America at the beginning of the Revolution, had arrived in Paris. Diaghilev soon made his acquaintance and, after hearing several of Dukelsky's early compositions, commissioned him to do the score for a ballet, the scenario for which he entrusted to me.

Since his discovery of Stravinsky and Prokofiev, Diaghilev had not worked with any other Russian composer, but he found Dukelsky extremely gifted and saw him as their direct successor. During performances of this new ballet, he used to present Dukelsky to the Paris press as his "third son," the first two being Stravinsky and Prokofiev. He predicted a great future for him, although he deplored the young composer's penchant for jazz, which he himself detested. When he talked to friends about Dukelsky, he would omit any mention of the composer's connection with variety shows and musical comedies in the United States, where Dukelsky was beginning to be known under the pseudonym Vernon Duke.

Diaghilev had a horror of jazz. He was a friend of Cole Porter, whose musical comedies were famous, but Diaghilev never talked to him about his music and pretended not to know that this charming, high-living "American in Paris" was a composer. He was aware, however, that with Princess Edmond de Polignac acting as go-between, Porter had asked Stravinsky to give him lessons in orchestration. Nothing came of it because Stravinsky demanded such an exorbitant fee. Then, in 1927, Diaghilev wrote me from Venice: "Cole is writing a ballet. . . . Danger!"

Shortly before one of my trips to Italy with Diaghilev, Cole Porter gave me a portable phonograph and a collection of dance and jazz records (none of his own composition). Diaghilev immediately replaced this "cabaret repertoire" with recordings of his "gods"— the Italian and Russian opera singers, Tamagno, Caruso, and Chaliapin.

One day, Cole Porter invited Diaghilev and me to lunch with George Gershwin, who was passing through Paris and wanted Diaghilev to hear his *Rhapsody in Blue*, which he would have loved to have performed by the Ballets Russes. Diaghilev listened in silence while Gershwin played his score, promised to "think about the question of using it for a ballet," but never gave him an answer.

Diaghilev was outraged by the jazz invasion of Europe and by its influence on young composers. In 1926, he wrote to me:

Dolin, by Pruna,
Monte Carlo, 1925

Saturday, August 7, 1926
Hôtel des Bains
Lido, Venice

. . . We have stopped at the Hôtel des Bains because the fracases at the Excelsior make life intolerable. The whole of Venice is up in arms against Cole Porter because of his jazz and his Negroes. He has started an idiotic night club on a boat moored opposite the Salute, and now the Grand Canal is swarming with the very same Negroes who have made us all run away from London and Paris. They are teaching the "Charleston" on the Lido beach! It's dreadful! The gondoliers are threatening to massacre all the elderly American women here. The very fact of their (Linda and Cole Porter's) renting the Palazzo Rezzonico is considered characteristic of nouveaux riches. Cole is greatly changed since his operation; he is thinner and appreciably older-looking.

In the twenty years of his company's existence, Diaghilev only once considered having an American composer collaborate on a ballet. That was during his preliminary talks in Venice with Otto Kahn and Morris Gest about a possible tour of the Ballets Russes in the United States. As a condition for such a tour, which in the end never did take place, Kahn stipulated that Diaghilev stage an American ballet, and Diaghilev agreed to present a work by John Alden Carpenter in New York.

Carpenter admired the Ballets Russes and had long hoped to see a ballet of his listed in the Diaghilev repertoire. He took an active part in working out the plans for an American tour, and, in 1924, I received a letter from Diaghilev, in which he said:

Detail from sketch by Pruna

July 19, 1924
Hotel Excelsior
Lido, Venice

As happens to me—always to me—I find myself at the Excelsior in unbelievable circumstances: I have met here no more nor less than Otto Kahn and Gatti-Casazza, the co-directors of the Metropolitan, Morris Gest (the impresario), Bodanzky (musical director at the Metropolitan), Max Reinhardt and Vollmöller (authors of The Miracle*), Scandiani (director of La Scala), and, on top of that, Carpenter turned up. He came over from America for two days, and he's just gone back, leaving me the score for his ballet.*

This whole crowd has assembled here to discuss forthcoming theatrical seasons in America. You can imagine the sensation my appearance created. Photographers sprang up on all sides and had us pose in "colorful groups," etc. . . .

Kahn rushed over to me and said point-blank that he would be very glad to "talk business" with me. . . . Carpenter's presence has been a great help in the present instance, for both Kahn and Gest find him a serious and important person. He has already begun to assist us.

Happily, his ballet is not as bad as I expected. It's not a "false-note," but rather, I'd say, it is American de Falla, with appropriate folklore. Also, the famous "policemen's strike" no longer takes place on the Strand but in an American factory, with alarm whistles and workers and such. Carpenter is asking whether the décor and all the rest couldn't be assigned to a Russian Bolshevik painter because, in his ballet, he is "not far from Bolshevism." I find this notion amusing. The Bolsheviks are wooing me, by the way. The catalogue of their exhibition here starts out with my name.

The Dukelsky ballet project was very close to Diaghilev's heart. He called it "his kindergarten," because he planned to assign the principal roles to the youngest premier danseur of the company, Anton Dolin, and to two tyros, Alice Nikitina and Serge Lifar, whereas the regular soloists of the Ballets Russes—Danilova, Sokolova, Tchernicheva, and Doubrovska—would dance in the corps de ballet. As for the authors of the ballet, Dukelsky and I were barely twenty.

In July, 1924, after Diaghilev had approved my plan for the scenario, I took off with Dukelsky for Choisel, in the Chevreuse Valley, to work on our ballet, which I had entitled *Zéphyr et Flore.* The company was on vacation, and Diaghilev had gone down to Venice. From his first letter on, he kept writing about Dukelsky, who claimed to be deluged with offers from theatre directors and music publishers:

July 19, 1924
Hotel Excelsior
Lido, Venice

. . . I think with interest about your ballet with Dima [Dukelsky]. However, Dima must not become the darling of the businessmen for a few months; they would drop him later, as they've done with Prokofiev. You will understand, I am sure, that were he to collaborate with the Swedish Ballet, under no circumstances would I compete with them, and I would not work with Dima, no matter what the project.

The next letters from Diaghilev all concerned *Zéphyr et Flore*. He was passionately interested in the slightest details of the ballet, and wanted to guide and help us:

Sunday, July 21, 1924
Hotel Excelsior
Lido, Venice

I've received your scenario. The apple orchard I like, as far as style is concerned. The sarafans [Russian peasant tunics] also, although in Russia, in the eighteenth century, Olympus was described quite otherwise, in a pompous, boring way. Remember Paisiello or the portrait of N. P. Scheremetiev costumed as Cupid, in Ostankino.

But, obviously, all this is not important. What does matter is that it will certainly be most difficult to explain choreographically where Zéphyr flies off to, and why. Among other things, in my opinion the very first dance of Zéphyr and Flore must be a pas de trois with Aeolus [Diaghilev is referring to Boreas]. That will be more original, and perhaps one will be better able to understand Aeolus's share in Zéphyr's departure. With whom will Flore dance her adagio? No men? Aeolus's scene must be full of seductiveness. It seems to me that Flore must be overcome not only by fear but also by the charm of Aeolus. The climax is utterly incomprehensible. Zéphyr falls—from where? why?—if the Fates are going to carry him? I don't know what to suggest. Would it not be better if he fell on the stage? Then the Fates can run up, thinking he has been killed. The ending is good. The absence of Aeolus is unfortunate; he should be puffing from somewhere! And the finale—is it to be danced?

These are my brief comments. In any event, this is a ballet that must be done. It hits the bull's-eye. But who is to do the mise-en-scène? A Russian? Braque?

Monday, July 22, 1924
Hotel Excelsior
Lido, Venice

As rearranged, the ballet remains almost the same. I still do not know where to put the pas de trois, whether in the second or the last number, but it is indispensable. The other directives I gave you yesterday remain unchanged.

Sketches from *Zéphyr et Flore*, by Georges Braque

I've just played the score. I like the music, provided it is as simple as your scenario. Actually, this is the most important thing. Pruna is simple, and therein lies his complexity. His painting is sweet but at the same time saltier than salt, yet even so it leaves one with a pleasant aftertaste of sugar.

Aeolus is at his best only when he resembles a drunkard heading for the police station. He is as gentle as a Negro and as ambiguous as the god Pan in that turquoise landscape, the most banal in the Adriatic.

I do not know whether Dima will understand this. But you must certainly understand it, for you understand everything; you are even, perhaps, too wise. With you, it's the same as with a wise dog—one never knows whether he is guided by his own intelligence or is obeying orders, whether he is guessing or, better yet, is acting on intuition. Paraphrase this for Dima, or read it to him.

At the moment, the sea before me is like the most banal of postcards and my soul is at peace.

P.S. Not long ago, an apple orchard would have suggested to Rimsky-Korsakov, or even to the young Stravinsky, a secret, mysterious place, an impenetrable jungle, whereas in our day the poet seeks an ordinary apple on Olympus, an apple without artifice or complications, which is the most flavorful kind. The simplest and soundest is the best.

The original notion for the staging of *Zéphyr et Flore* envisaged it in the form of a dramatic performance being presented in the private theatre of a Russian nobleman in the days of serfdom; the performers would be a troupe of serfs—young peasants disguised

Serge Lifar in 1924

Lifar in *Zéphyr et Flore*

as mythological divinities. With the commissioning of such a mise-en-scène in mind, Diaghilev made a tour of the studios of young Russian painters in Paris and London, but he found no one who seemed appropriate. He relinquished his vision of a rustic Russian Olympus and turned to Georges Braque.

For the 1925 production of *Zéphyr et Flore* in Monte Carlo, Braque provided a single set for the ballet's action, but later, at Diaghilev's request, he expanded his décor with two additional backdrops. He had come down to Monte Carlo in April, when the finishing touches were being put on *Zéphyr et Flore*; his visit coincided with the inauguration of the Casino's Salle Ganne, originally intended for chamber-music recitals but converted by Diaghilev into a theatre for ballet. Diaghilev thought of it as the experimental theatre for his company, where he presented dance recitals, entrusting the roles currently performed by his premiers danseurs to the young hopefuls of the troupe—Alicia Markova, Ninette de Valois, Alice Nikitina, Dolin, Lifar, Constantin Tcherkas. For one of these performances, Braque designed a new set for *Sylphides*, but he forbade Diaghilev to use it elsewhere.

The question of the choreography for *Zéphyr et Flore* concerned Diaghilev greatly. Nijinska was still official choreographer of the Ballets Russes, but her relationship with Diaghilev had grown increasingly strained ever since he had engaged Balanchine as a member of the company.

Balanchine had joined the company as a dancer, and up to that time he had not choreographed a ballet for Diaghilev. Nonetheless, Nijinska sensed a rival in this newcomer, and her hostility toward him was quite apparent. She also disapproved of Diaghilev's infatuation with Lifar, whom she considered less gifted a dancer than the other students she had brought from Russia at the same time.

For his part, Diaghilev was exasperated by Nijinska's stubborn, authoritarian character. Remembering the complications that had attended the creation of *Le Train Bleu*, he longed to find a new and young choreographer who would be capable of replacing Nijinska as quickly as possible.

Dolin and Nikitina in *Zéphyr et Flore*

Because he did not know any substantial choreographic work by Balanchine, Diaghilev hesitated to trust him with *Zéphyr et Flore*. So, after patiently explaining to Lifar the problems of contemporary dance and of creating a ballet, he decided to test his capacities as a choreographer. To spare Lifar criticism from the company, Diaghilev chose two of Lifar's friends to help work out his first choreographic efforts and, unbeknownst to Nijinska and the other dancers, had them work in a private studio. But, after attending one rehearsal, during which Lifar struggled in vain to devise a pas de deux for *Zéphyr et Flore*, Diaghilev lost his illusions; he made his peace with Massine, and engaged him as choreographer for the ballet.

On the eve of the dress rehearsal in Monte Carlo, Diaghilev was the image of despair. He was disappointed with Massine's mechanical, cold, and dry choreography and with Dukelsky's unprofessional orchestration, which so distorted the music as to make it unrecognizable. As for Braque's costumes, aside from those for the three principal dancers they seemed to have been designed to produce a comic effect, and the women wept as they waited in the wings to appear onstage in such regalia.

These flaws were irreparable, moreover, for Massine had left Monte Carlo the moment he finished his job—"fulfilled the contract and delivered the goods"—without worrying about the fate of his ballet. Dukelsky, convinced of his gifts as an orchestrator, was shunning Diaghilev to avoid hearing his criticisms and being forced to revise the score.

When the set was assembled onstage, Braque spent hours sitting alone in the empty theatre, gravely contemplating it, but he seemed curiously indifferent to the disastrous costumes. Having made certain that they conformed to his sketches, he declared himself satisfied and bothered no more about them.

Diaghilev grew more somber daily, afraid that *Zéphyr et Flore* would be a failure. His disappointment and rage reached a peak at the close of the dress rehearsal—which was an unexpected success—for as Lifar, whose presence dominated the ballet, leaped offstage, he bumped into Danilova in the wings, and sprained his ankle, thereby forcing the cancellation of the première of *Zéphyr et Flore*.

LES MATELOTS

Ballet in five scenes by Boris Kochno. Music by Georges Auric. Choreography by Leonide Massine. Curtains, décor, and costumes by Pedro Pruna. First performance: Théâtre de la Gaîté-Lyrique, Paris, June 17, 1925.

In 1924, when Auric was beginning to compose the music for *Les Matelots* (its original title had been *Les Marins*), Jean Cocteau talked to me enthusiastically about the paintings of a young Catalan artist whom he had met at Picasso's studio. His name was Pedro Pruna. Shortly thereafter, Pruna came to call on us—Diaghilev and me—at the Hôtel Savoy in Paris, and showed us photographs of his canvases. Inspired by Picasso's "Ingres period," they promised a limpid, poetic theatrical work.

Diaghilev commissioned Pruna to design the sets and costumes for *Les Matelots*. When the ballet was in rehearsal, he had Pruna come to London and to Monte Carlo, where Pruna painted the portraits of several Ballets Russes members, but he was unable to do one of

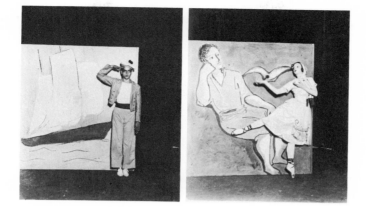

Lifar in *Les Matelots*

Sketch by Pruna

Diaghilev, who had refused, after leaving Russia, to pose for any painter.

It had been Diaghilev's intention to ask Nijinska to create the choreography for *Les Matelots*, but the proposals she submitted seemed to him too realistic. He gave up the idea of her collaborating on it, and turned to Massine.

In agreeing to do the choreography, Massine objected violently to my idea that the ballet should be danced by five principals only; he insisted on a group of secondary dancers. He was deaf to all my arguments and finally managed to convince Diaghilev that he should be permitted to include the whole corps de ballet. After attending one rehearsal, however, Diaghilev disapproved of the "overpopulated" version of the ballet, and on leaving the studio, he said to Massine, "This ballet is written for five people and it will be danced by five people. Not one more!"

Nonetheless, during the London performances of *Les Matelots*, Diaghilev did add an additional character. He introduced onstage a one-legged street musician who habitually played outside the theatre entrance, where the line for inexpensive seats queued up. This was a virtuoso whose percussion instrument was a pair of spoons.

The theatrical debut of this mountebank created a sensation, and the next morning all the London papers published his photograph, captioned "Street Musician's Romance. From Kerbstone to Russian Ballet." One paper went on to say: "George Peter Dines, an ex-Service man who played tunes in the London streets on spoons, plates and cigar boxes, is now giving his spoon performance in 'Les Matelots.'"

At the Paris dress rehearsal of *Les Matelots*, an unplanned incident was applauded by the audience as an inspired bit of stage business.

In the fourth scene—in a bar—wooden chairs were the sailors' partners; they danced with them and then sat down on them. The rickety chair brandished by Lifar could not support his weight and when, at the end of the dance, he collapsed onto it, the chair also collapsed. His tumble happened to coincide with the final note of the music; the audience took this as an intentional comic effect, and it produced an ovation.

BARABAU

Ballet with chorus of singers. Libretto and music by Vittorio Rieti. Choreography by George Balanchine. Décor and costumes by Maurice Utrillo. First performance: Coliseum Theatre, London, December 11, 1925.

Darius Milhaud was the first person to draw Diaghilev's attention to the music of a young Italian composer, Vittorio Rieti, and in particular to a brief a cappella choral composition entitled *Barabau*. Soon thereafter, in August, 1925, Diaghilev met Rieti in Venice. He listened to Rieti's ballet *Noah's Ark*, the scenario of which he disliked because it only included animal roles, but he commissioned Rieti to compose a folkloristic ballet score based on his *Barabau*.

Diaghilev knew no young Italian painters whose work would suit Rieti's music, so he decided to approach Maurice Utrillo.

Utrillo was living in the country at the time, and the only way to get in touch with him was through André Utter, the young husband of Suzanne Valadon, the artist's mother. Utter, himself a painter, attended to the family's business affairs; it was he who accepted commissions for paintings and wrestled with buyers over terms.

When Diaghilev had reached an agreement with Utter, he decided to send me to see Utrillo in the country and talk with him about *Barabau.* One rainy October morning, I arrived at the Château St. Bernard, not far from Paris, where Utrillo was living, and I spent the day with Utter and Valadon.

I saw—or, rather, I was allowed to see—Utrillo for a few minutes only. Valadon and Utter led me into a large, dark, and empty room on the ground floor, which must have served as his studio. There, sitting on a kitchen chair, he was awaiting my visit. Tall and thin, dressed in corduroy peasant trousers and jacket, Utrillo seemed unwell; his gentle, melancholy eyes were often vacant. He listened indifferently as I spoke about the ballet; it was enough for him to know that he was being asked to paint "a landscape with a church," and no further details seemed to interest him.

Utrillo emerged from his torpor only once, on learning that among the ballet costumes he was to design there should be one for an Italian soldier. He seemed to be at a loss and was becoming agitated, whereupon his mother intervened and advised him to copy the uniform of the village gendarme.

Diaghilev never met Utrillo, and the painter never saw the ballet for which he designed the mise-en-scène. Their relations were limited to two letters in which Utrillo sought to recover from Diaghilev part of the payment owed him by the Ballets Russes as well as the sketches for the sets and costumes for *Barabau.* The first letter from Utrillo, dated March 18, 1928, was friendly and, apart from the question of money, spoke of the triumphs of the Ballets Russes and the agreeable climate of the Côte d'Azur. But, a month later, having received no answer from Diaghilev, who seemed to have forgotten his debt, Utrillo changed his tune and forcefully demanded what was owed him.

After receiving this demand, Diaghilev undertook to calm Utrillo's rage, sending him the sketches and the three thousand francs, which erased the debt.

Despite the success of *Barabau,* Diaghilev was obliged to remove it from the repertoire of the company because of the production difficulties created by the inclusion of the chorus.

Lifar in *Barabau*

Lydia Sokolova
and Léon Woizikowski
in *Barabau*

ROMEO AND JULIET

A rehearsal without scenery, in two acts. Music by Constant Lambert. Choreography by Bronislava Nijinska. Décor by Max Ernst and Joan Miró. First performance: Casino, Monte Carlo, May 4, 1926. First performance in Paris: Théâtre Sarah Bernhardt, May 18, 1926.

In 1925, London friends of Diaghilev who followed closely developments in the arts were beginning to talk about two "white hopes" of English music—the young composers Constant Lambert and William Walton, whose names were coupled as were those of Auric and Poulenc in Paris.

On principle, Diaghilev questioned the musical genius of the English and had never sought the collaboration of English composers. However, after he had attended a concert at which early works by Lambert were played (this concert presenting new musicians was called, I believe, "Promenades"), he found his music "danceable," and commissioned him to write a ballet score. As for Walton, in the program of musical entr'actes for the 1926 Ballets Russes season in London, Diaghilev included his overture for orchestra that had been inspired by Rowlandson's etching, "Portsmouth Point."

Lifar in
Romeo and Juliet,
1926

Lifar and Karsavina
in *Romeo and Juliet*,
Paris, 1926

When Diaghilev asked Lambert to compose a ballet score, he had no definite scenario to propose and suggested that he take his inspiration from some gouaches by an anonymous primitive artist, probably a nineteenth-century British seaman, which we had seen in Augustus John's studio. In November, 1925, Lambert wrote to Diaghilev from London to say that John had agreed to design the ballet's mise-en-scène (for which he asked me to write a scenario) and would take these gouaches as a basis.

This project did not materialize, however, and in 1926 I wrote a scenario for Lambert's ballet that was a choreographic version of *Romeo and Juliet*. It was divided into two parts: first, the studio rehearsal of some scenes from the Shakespeare play; then the actual performance, which ended with the flight of the two principals. Although at the time the score for *Romeo and Juliet* was to be published (the Ballets Russes kept the English spelling from the outset), Lambert wrote me asking permission to use my name as author of the scenario, I refused, in agreement with Diaghilev, who at that point wanted to present his ballet as the work of young, exclusively English artists.

For the *Romeo and Juliet* set, Diaghilev spoke to Christopher Wood, a young painter whom we had known in London through a mutual friend, Antonio de Gandarillas. Wood happened to be in Monte Carlo that spring, and after reaching an agreement with Diaghilev, he began work at once on the sketches for the first scene, which was to consist only of a series of mirrors and practice barres.

However, on a trip to Paris, Diaghilev discovered the Surrealist movement. He met Max Ernst and Joan Miró, visited their studios, and, abandoning his idea of an "English ballet" and of Wood's collaboration, he ordered the *Romeo and Juliet* designs from them.

The idea of seeing a Surrealist production of his ballet horrified Lambert, who had heard the news through Wood; from London, he wired and then wrote Diaghilev to dissuade him from this new plan. Lambert's messages—angry, inept, and despairing—went unanswered.

Arriving in Monte Carlo for the final rehearsals of *Romeo and Juliet*, Lambert still hoped to make Diaghilev change his mind. He would pursue him in the street and, when he was not received at the Hôtel de Paris, would wait for Diaghilev at the entrance. But, for all Lambert's supplications and his threatening to forbid the performance of his ballet, Diaghilev's decision was irrevocable.

After some thought of getting a young English choreographer for *Romeo and Juliet*, Diaghilev ended by engaging Nijinska, who had not been a member of the company since 1924. Her return was not a success. She took off from the premise that she was choreographing a dramatic work, and, by undertaking simply to substitute gestures for words she repeated for the greater part of the ballet the error she had made with *Les Fâcheux* and foundered in a conventional, realistic pantomime. Thanks to the magic of Karsavina's presence and the youthful, masculine charm of Lifar, the ballet met with success in Monte

Carlo; in Paris, for unforeseeable reasons, it precipitated a clamorous scandal.

André Breton and Louis Aragon, the leaders of the Surrealist movement, to which both Ernst and Miró belonged, disapproved of their participating in Diaghilev's capitalistic enterprise, and they attempted to sabotage the Paris première of *Romeo and Juliet*. They deployed their young followers among the audience at the Sarah Bernhardt, and when the curtain rose to reveal Miró's décor, these young partisans of Surrealism unleashed an indescribable hubbub and showered the audience with copies of a proclamation that read:

PROTEST! *It is inadmissible that thought should be at the beck and call of money. Yet not one year goes by but that some man one has believed incorruptible surrenders to the very powers he has until then opposed. Those individuals who capitulate to the point of disregarding social conditions are of no importance, for the ideal to which they paid allegiance before their abdication survives without them. In this sense, the participation of Max Ernst and Joan Miró in the next performance of the Ballets Russes can never involve the Surrealist ideal in their debasement. That ideal is essentially subversive; it cannot compromise with such enterprises, whose aim has always been to tame the dreams and rebellions engendered by physical and intellectual starvation for the benefit of an international aristocracy.*

It may have seemed to Ernst and Miró that their collaboration with M. de Diaghilev, legitimized by the example of Picasso, would not have such serious consequences. However, it forces us whose main concern is to keep the outposts of the intellect beyond the grasp of slave traders of every kind—it forces us, without regard for individuals, to denounce an attitude that supplies weapons to the worst partisans of moral equivocation.

It is well known that we attach relatively little importance to our artistic affinities with this person or that. May the public grant us the honor of believing that in May, 1926, we are more than ever unable to sacrifice our own sense of revolutionary reality.

Louis Aragon, André Breton

Joan Miró and
Max Ernst,
Monte Carlo, 1926

The manifesto was printed in red ink. While the leaflets were tossed from the upper balconies, inundating the audience seated in the orchestra, Louis Aragon perched on the handrail of a box in the top tier and harangued the spectators, who were shouting back for fear he would come hurtling down on their heads. Among other incidents in the course of the riot, Lady Abdy was observed seizing the trumpet one of the demonstrators was blowing, whereupon, in revenge, he grabbed the top of her dress and unclothed her.

When the hullabaloo began, Serge Grigoriev, the company's regisseur, acting on Diaghilev's orders, had the curtain lowered and stopped the performance. It was resumed only after the police had intervened and the demonstrators had been driven out of the theatre. The "Surrealist scandal" whetted the curiosity of Parisians about *Romeo and Juliet* and increased to the maximum box-office receipts for the Diaghilev productions.

LA
PASTORALE

Ballet in twelve scenes by Boris Kochno. Music by Georges Auric. Choreography by George Balanchine. Décor and costumes by Pedro Pruna. First performance: Théâtre Sarah Bernhardt, Paris, May 29, 1926.

The successful collaboration of Auric, Pruna, and myself in creating *Les Matelots* encouraged Diaghilev to bring us together once more to produce a new ballet, *La Pastorale*. From the earlier crew who worked on *Les Matelots*, only Massine was absent, having been replaced by Balanchine, but our common labor on *La Pastorale* did not result in any success comparable to the preceding year's.

Despite many happy inspirations in the solo dances, Balanchine's choreography lacked substance. The action was confused, and the plot, based on antic situations that arise between some screen actors and villagers acting as extras in a film being shot outdoors, was incomprehensible to the audience.

However, the stars of *La Pastorale* were unforgettable. Lifar's entrance on a bicycle was a sensation, and Doubrovska, who until then had been considered a purely classical dancer, showed herself to be a remarkable interpreter of contemporary ballet.

Costume design for *La Pastorale*, by Pruna

JACK IN THE BOX

Dances by Erik Satie, orchestrated by Darius Milhaud. Choreography by George Balanchine. Décor and costumes by André Derain. First performance: Théâtre Sarah Bernhardt, Paris, June 3, 1926.

In the autumn of 1922, when Diaghilev was planning his opera season in Monte Carlo, he learned that Satie was writing an opera based on Bernardin de Saint-Pierre's novel *Paul et Virginie*, which Cocteau and Radiguet had adapted for the stage. Satie intended his score for the Théâtre des Champs-Élysées, of which Hébertot was then director. Cocteau, however, knew of Diaghilev's project to found a permanent opera company, and wanted *Paul et Virginie* to be done by this group. On October 24, 1922, he wrote to Diaghilev:

I don't at all forget you. Paul is on Hébertot's program poster—but he is arranging for the work to pass from him to you. Satie is so difficult to cope with that I am waiting for the right moment. This can be at table or while I'm shaving in the morning in my bedroom and he is trimming his beard with my nail scissors. You would reimburse the advance (paid to Satie by Hébertot) and the trick will be turned.

Diaghilev's lack of success with his opera season in Monte Carlo made him give up his opera projects; he lost interest in *Paul et Virginie*, and reminded Satie of his intention to write a new ballet.

In 1922, Diaghilev had commissioned Satie to write the score for a ballet on a theme conceived by André Derain. Derain had already prepared sketches for the costumes, and on December 4, 1922, after a conversation with him, Satie wrote to Diaghilev: "I have seen Derain. I'd not been familiar with his sketches for the characters. Amusing, no? Yes. We shall see about this, and I shall be pleased to talk with you Wednesday."

The completion of this project was delayed, however, because Diaghilev was working intensively on the organization of the Monte Carlo opera season, scheduled for January, 1924. In the repertoire for this season, he had included an opéra comique by Gounod, *Le Médecin Malgré Lui*, for which he asked Satie to write recitatifs or, rather, as Satie put it in his contract with Diaghilev, "to compose supplementary scenes, not written by Gounod, for the latter's work."

While Satie was composing his recitatifs, he often met with Diaghilev and closely followed his suggestions for the music. On December 14, 1923, he wrote to Diaghilev:

My dear good Director:

I look everywhere, I do not see you. Where is it "that you are"? Yes.

The third act is almost finished. I'm up to No. 9. Much pleased with my work. Pretty,

Diaghilev,
1925 or 1926

plump, elegant, delicate, superior, exquisite, varied, melancholy, extra . . . etc., . . . such is this, my work, fruit of my diurnal, even my nocturnal (but rarely), vigils.

I love you still, and admire you increasingly. Yes. Come back quickly.

Yours,

E.S.

The work in progress for the opera season notwithstanding, Satie did not relinquish the idea for a new ballet, and after one luncheon, which was abruptly cut short, probably to Diaghilev's surprise, Satie sent him a wildly absurd wire in which he mentioned a forth-coming meeting with Derain:

ARCUEIL, JUNE 3, 1923: MY DEAR AND MOST EXQUISITE DIRECTOR—FORGIVE MY ABRUPT DEPARTURE THIS AFTERNOON. . . . IF YOU KNEW WHAT HAPPENED TO ME! . . . A HORROR! . . . YES . . . I BLUSH FOR IT. . . . I WAS ALL OF A SUDDEN SEIZED BY ONE OF THOSE VAST AND PROFOUND ATTACKS OF COLIC THAT UNDO A MAN. . . . AM UNDONE STILL, AND INDIGNANT. . . . FORGIVE ME, PLEASE. . . . LET US FORGET THIS DETAIL. I WILL GO TOMORROW TO SEE DERAIN. WE MEET SOON AGAIN RE GOUNOD, NO? . . . YOURS, E.S.

Danilova
and Idzikowski in
Jack in the Box

In the spring of 1924, at the conclusion of his Monte Carlo opera season, Diaghilev again commissioned the ballet from Satie. (At that point, Satie was writing him, "Long live the Ballets Russes! Down with the Théâtre de Monte Carlo!")

Renouncing his collaboration with Derain, Diaghilev asked Georges Braque to design the sets and costumes for the ballet Satie had agreed to compose for the Ballets Russes, which was to be called *Quadrille*. (The idea for this commission had been suggested to Diaghilev by a Chabrier quadrille based on various Wagnerian operatic melodies.)

Despite repeated promises, Satie never delivered the score for *Quadrille*, although, in the course of 1924, he did discuss the project with Braque.

After Satie's death in 1925, Darius Milhaud was cataloguing his papers when he dis-covered the unpublished manuscript of three pieces for piano entitled "Jack in the Box," which he orchestrated and which Diaghilev used as the score for the ballet of the same name.

Diaghilev commissioned Derain to design the sets and costumes for this dance diver-tissement, and the artist specified the date on which they would be ready. When Diaghilev and I came to his house to pick up the designs, Derain shut himself up in his studio on the pretext of looking for them among his other sketches. After we had waited for an hour in the entrance hall, he opened the studio door, and inside we found, spread over the floor, the water colors he had just finished. We carried them off with us still damp.

These drawings, together with those for several other ballets that are now in the col-lection of the Wadsworth Atheneum, in Hartford, Connecticut, Diaghilev gave to Lifar, for whom, in the last years of his life, he put together a collection of paintings by contempo-rary artists, as he had done for Massine ten years earlier. (Diaghilev organized an exhibit of the Massine collection in Rome, in 1917, and of the Lifar collection in London, in 1926.)

At the time of Diaghilev's death, the Lifar collection was stored in Paris, in an apart-ment on the Boulevard Garibaldi leased in Diaghilev's name and mine. As co-tenant, I had free access to the apartment, which made it possible for me to return to Lifar his collection, which was in danger of being dispersed at public auction, as were all Diaghilev's possessions.

THE TRIUMPH OF NEPTUNE

English pantomime in twelve scenes. Libretto by Sacheverell Sitwell. Music by Lord Berners. Choreography by George Balanchine. Sets and costumes adapted and executed by Prince A. Schervashidze from prints by George and Robert Cruikshank, Tofts, Honigold, and Webb, collected by B. Pollock and H. J. Webb. First performance: Lyceum Theatre, London, December 3, 1926. First Paris performance: Théâtre Sarah Bernhardt, May 27, 1927.

Ln producing an English ballet, *The Triumph of Neptune*, Diaghilev wished to pay tribute to Lord Rothermere, whose financial assistance had enabled him to present in 1926, at His Majesty's Theatre, one of the most brilliant of the Ballets Russes seasons.

Diaghilev was bringing to fruition an old project when, in 1926, he commissioned Lord Berners to compose a ballet score. They had met some years earlier, in Rome, where, be-

Costume designs for *The Triumph of Neptune*, by Pruna

fore the composer inherited the family name and title from his uncle, he had been a member of the British diplomatic corps under his given name of Gerald Tyrwhitt. As early as his June, 1919, ballet season in London, Diaghilev had presented pieces by Berners in the course of the symphonic entr'actes conducted by Eugene Goossens.

Relations between the two men were cordial. One day, when Diaghilev was urging Berners to finish one variation for *Neptune*, the composer, who was a great art collector, wrote to him: "I don't feel too inspired at the moment. However, this morning I bought a very pretty Renoir, and hope that now things will go better."

Some years before this, Diaghilev and I had discovered a shop in the outskirts of London that sold engravings of the Victorian era; they represented fairy characters and settings intended for children's theatre productions.

Now, preferring not to have English painters work on the mise-en-scène for the new ballet, Diaghilev remembered these engravings and decided to use them as the basis for sets and costumes.

The print shop, owned first by J. Reddington and then by B. Pollock, was located in the old section of Hoxton and seemed not to have changed for almost a hundred years. In the semidarkness of this shop I spent whole days with Diaghilev, shuffling through dusty piles of countless engravings of such pantomime sets as "Jack the Giant Killer," "The Forty Thieves," and "The Silver Palace."

Scenes from
The Triumph of Neptune

Pedro Pruna, although he did not sign his sketches, designed the costumes for *The Triumph of Neptune* after figures in these engravings. When the costumes were being executed, Diaghilev completed them with tiaras and gem-encrusted breastplates from nineteenth-century pantomime wardrobes we had discovered among the old stocks of London costumers.

The poet Sacheverell Sitwell, who wrote the scenario for *Neptune*, shared actively in our researches and rounded out our own findings with other illustrations from the same period. He became so enthusiastic over these engravings that he kept adding new episodes to his ballet, until finally it included twelve scenes. During its London performances, the ballet lasted so long and the scene shiftings were so complicated that Diaghilev decided to abridge it and to present only ten scenes in Paris.

The elimination of one scene was not the result of a spontaneous decision on Diaghilev's part, however, but was caused by the intervention of the Monte Carlo Casino management, who, alarmed by the increase in suicides among unlucky players, begged Diaghilev to withdraw a scene in which a ballet character hanged himself.

The Triumph of Neptune was the last ballet in which Balanchine danced with the Diaghilev company; he took part in the "Pas des Arlequins" and later gave a remarkable interpretation in the role of the Negro, Snowball.

LA CHATTE

Ballet in one act by Sobeka, after an Aesop fable. Music by Henri Sauguet. Choreography by George Balanchine. Architectural and sculptural constructions by Naum Gabo and Antoine Pevsner. First performance: Casino, Monte Carlo, April 30, 1927. First performance in Paris: Théâtre Sarah Bernhardt, May 27, 1927.

Spessivtzeva,
Paris, 1927

Ever since hearing Henri Sauguet's opéra bouffe, *Le Plumet du Colonel*, which the company of Mme. Beriza presented at the Théâtre des Champs-Élysées in 1924, Diaghilev had taken an interest in the young musician's work, and presently decided to commission him to write a ballet score. He was encouraged in this by the fact that Roger Desormière, who had become orchestral director for the Ballets Russes in 1925, was most enthusiastic about Sauguet's work. Both men belonged to the École d'Arcueil, a group of young musicians who were disciples of Erik Satie, and Desormière considered Sauguet the new hope of French music; he used to refer to him as "the young Bizet."

As he was elaborating his work plan, Sauguet first thought of asking Paul Éluard to write the scenario; then, deciding that Éluard's collaboration would be "too dangerous," he approached René Crevel. But Diaghilev was eager to involve Spessivtzeva in the creation of a contemporary work, and what he was looking for was simply a theme that offered a "pretext for dancing." He settled on the adaptation I had made of an Aesop fable about the cat who was changed into a woman.

I called my ballet *La Chatte* and signed the scenario with a pseudonym—Sobeka—which contained the first consonants of my own and the other collaborators' names: *S* for Sauguet, *B* for Balanchine, and *K* for Kochno. The pseudonym had another meaning. Diaghilev often used to say that I was his faithful watchdog. In Russian, the word for "dog" is "*sobaka*"—just one letter away from my new pseudonym.

Commissioning the décor for *La Chatte* seemed to pose no problem, for Sauguet wanted the mise-en-scène to be entrusted to a friend of his, the painter Christian Bérard.

Sketches by Gabo and Pevsner

Spessivtzeva
and Lifar in
La Chatte, 1927

251

Spessivtzeva in
La Chatte

I had met Bérard at the home of my friend Pavel Tchelitchev, but was not familiar with his painting, and it was Jean Cocteau who first spoke of him to Diaghilev as the coming great painter and stage designer. Unhappily, Cocteau, wishing to rival Diaghilev's gifts as a "discoverer," insisted too emphatically on the fact that Bérard was "his discovery." This only irritated Diaghilev and made him hostile to Bérard even before they met.

The meeting itself was uncomfortable and disappointing. Sauguet took us to the eminently bourgeois town house of the painter's father, which in no way resembled the setting in which Diaghilev's imagination placed every young, unknown artist. He had never forgotten his first visit to Picasso's studio—ramshackle and freezing cold, with a window overlooking the Montparnasse cemetery—and from that day forth, Diaghilev appeared to believe that wretched quarters guaranteed their inhabitant's genius. Walking with me through the streets of Paris after a performance, Diaghilev, when he noticed a lighted dormer window, would say, "Who knows, perhaps a great artist is working up there whom we will never meet!"

The day of our visit, Bérard was intimidated by Diaghilev's presence and was in an indescribable state of nerves. He seemed to shy away from talking about painting or showing his own work. It was only when Diaghilev lost patience and got up to leave that Bérard brought himself to fetch a few small canvases to the conservatory, where he was receiving us. Apparently unfinished, they represented some melancholy characters—street acrobats in dirty tights, youths on crutches lounging in front of brick walls, and so on. Not one of these somber, austere paintings gave any hint of Bérard's genius as a designer or corresponded in the slightest to Diaghilev's theatrical concepts.

Diaghilev was annoyed by this awkward reception and also found Bérard's easel painting unadaptable to the stage, so he gave up any idea of working with him. Without con-

Constructivist set by Gabo and Pevsner

sulting Sauguet, he entrusted the scenic part of his ballet to two Russian sculptors, Naum Gabo and Antoine Pevsner, whose abstract work seemed the antithesis of the simple, limpid music of *La Chatte*. Sauguet was disconcerted by Diaghilev's choice and urged him to change his mind and to approach some realist painter. But Diaghilev was inflexible; he said he did not want the setting for this ballet to be like some concierge's hovel.

To build the set for *La Chatte* was no easy matter. Gabo and Pevsner had to construct the metal sections themselves. When they descended on the tranquil small hotels and family pensions of Monaco and set themselves up to do their welding, they aroused a general panic and put the regular guests to flight. No sooner would the management see them roaming the halls with blow torches, wearing weird safety masks that made them look like deep-sea divers, and hear the hellish noise that reverberated in their rooms than they were thrown out.

La Chatte was a tremendous success, thanks to several factors—the ingenious choreography of Balanchine; the luminous presence and poetic interpretation of Spessivtzeva, who was vigorously partnered by Lifar; the novelty of the décor; and the melodic score, brilliantly orchestrated by Sauguet.

However, the contretemps over the set created a strain in the relationship between Diaghilev and the young composer. Sauguet was extremely nervous and touchy, which irritated and finally infuriated Diaghilev. At the close of the first performance, the audience gave *La Chatte* a resounding ovation, and Sauguet, meeting Diaghilev in the wings, said to him, "You hear? . . . What a success!" To which Diaghilev replied, dryly, "Yes. And I am vastly surprised!"

On the eve of the Paris première, Spessivtzeva injured her leg and was replaced by Alice Nikitina, who thereafter alternated with Alicia Markova in the role of the Cat.

Markova in
La Chatte, 1927

Scene from *La Chatte*

OEDIPUS REX

Opera oratorio in two acts, after Sophocles. Text by Jean Cocteau, translated into Latin by J. Daniélou. Music by Igor Stravinsky. First public performance: Théâtre Sarah Bernhardt, Paris, June, 1927.

As early as the spring of 1926, Diaghilev was busy with the organization of his Paris season for the following year, which would mark the twentieth anniversary of his artistic enterprise in Paris. Personally, he attached no great importance to the anniversary. It only depressed him by reminding him of his age but he exploited it as a publicity theme for his 1927 season, and stressed it in order to persuade Stravinsky to write a new ballet.

Stravinsky had given up working on theatrical projects in 1923, but when Diaghilev insisted, he gave in and promised to write him a new piece for his "jubilee." He refused, however, to divulge either the plot of his new work or the style of its composition, saying that he wanted to give Diaghilev a surprise.

For months Diaghilev waited impatiently for Stravinsky to finish his work, and then, one day in Monte Carlo, he received a message inviting him to come to Nice, where Stravinsky was living at the time, to hear the new score.

I saw Diaghilev leave Monte Carlo one morning, radiant and smiling, and return from Nice in the evening troubled and perplexed. Stravinsky's surprise was *Oedipus Rex*, an opera oratorio in two acts, written in Latin; scenically, it was a static work, having no relation whatever to the dance.

Despite his disappointment, Diaghilev presented *Oedipus Rex* during the 1927 Paris season, and waited one year before he was able to produce a new ballet by Stravinsky, which was *Apollon Musagète*.

MERCURE

Plastic poses. Theme and choreography by Leonide Massine. Music by Erik Satie. Décor and costumes by Pablo Picasso. First performance: At *Les Soirées de Paris*, presented by Count Étienne de Beaumont, Théâtre de la Cigale, Paris, June 15, 1924. First performance by the Ballets Russes: Théâtre Sarah Bernhardt, Paris, June 2, 1927.

In the autumn of 1923, Jean Cocteau informed Diaghilev that Count Étienne de Beaumont, a devotee of modern art and a moving spirit in Parisian society, was organizing at the Théâtre de la Cigale a series of productions, for the most part dance performances, to be called *Les Soirées de Paris*.

Diaghilev was on friendly terms with Beaumont, who always invited him to his luxurious town house on rue Masseran. This was an eighteenth-century mansion (it had once been the Spanish Embassy), where Beaumont gave musical evenings and costume balls that were famous in their day. His new enterprise, however, was commercial, and it both surprised and alarmed Diaghilev, and made him look on Beaumont as a rival. This reaction was reinforced by the fact that several of the *Soirées de Paris* productions bore the names of some of Diaghilev's closest collaborators; what's more, the leading dancers of the new company were Lopoukhova and Idzikowski and the ballet master was Massine, all deserters from his own group.

The poster announcing *Les Soirées de Paris* prompted Diaghilev to say, "It's a Ballets Russes season where only my name is missing."

While preparing for his 1924 season, Diaghilev intervened with several members of his crew to dissuade them from taking part in the Beaumont enterprise or, at the very least, to limit their participation to dramatic works. Their response was uniformly reassuring,

Boris Kochno,
Diaghilev,
Baroness de Mayer,
Misia Sert,
Baron de Mayer,
Lido, Venice, 1921

yet nonetheless all of them, except Stravinsky, collaborated on *Les Soirées de Paris*.

Beaumont hoped to produce a ballet with choreography by Massine and décor by Picasso, using the score of Stravinsky's Octet. Stravinsky refused, however; he said his symphonic work stood by itself and needed no plastic presentation.

Braque, who had just completed the mise-en-scène for Diaghilev's *Les Fâcheux*, accepted a commission from Beaumont to do sets and costumes for *Salade*, a ballet by Darius Milhaud. "But," he wrote to Diaghilev in March, 1924, "to prevent *Les Fâcheux* and *Salade* from hurting one another, I have made an arrangement that is to your advantage. Your ballet will be produced first." Nevertheless, *Salade* was presented in Paris on May 17, 1924, while the première of *Les Fâcheux* did not take place until June 4.

Massine and Lissanevich in *Mercure*

As for Cocteau, he wrote to Diaghilev in Monte Carlo on February 29, 1924:

I was desolate not to have been able to say good-bye. I wanted to fill you in about one of the Cigale projects that will please you, I imagine, because it greatly alters the aspect of the whole enterprise.

É. de Beaumont is asking me to stage Roméo et Juliette, *to alternate with his music-hall program. I am collaborating with Jean V. Hugo, and I'm having some Scottish bagpipers brought over from England.*

So I am doing nothing that is in any way like your productions, and am confining myself to theatre *theatre.*

In regard to Picasso, who at that very moment was working on the mise-en-scène for *Mercure*, Cocteau added: "I have seen Picasso. He's working. He is amazed at your taking umbrage, and speaks of you and of your ballet with complete friendliness."

Although Diaghilev was not invited, he attended the opening performance of *Les Soirées de Paris*. His apprehensions were straightaway quieted, when he realized the dilettantism of Beaumont's undertaking, which created a stir only in fashionable circles. Yet when the production of *Mercure* provoked violent protests from the audience, he was the first to express his admiration for the work of Satie and Picasso.

Beaumont's Paris programs ran for only one season, and presently he renewed his connection with Diaghilev. In 1926, he turned over to the Ballets Russes the music for *Jack in the Box*, for which he held performance rights (as I have mentioned, Milhaud had discovered among Satie's papers the manuscript score of this suite, which Satie thought he had lost on a bus), as well as all the scenic and musical materials of *Mercure*.

Mercure became part of the Diaghilev repertoire, but was performed only in Paris and London. Apprehensive about the reactions of the English critics to the violence of Picasso's work, Diaghilev gave the press no advance notice of the new ballet and billed it for a single matinee performance.

ODE

An evening meditation on the Majesty of God on observing the Aurora Borealis

Spectacle in three acts. Scenic book by Boris Kochno. Music by Nicholas Nabokov, words by Mikhail Lomonosov. Decorative elements by Pavel Tchelitchev, in collaboration with Pierre Charbonnier. Choreography by
Leonide Massine. First performance: Théâtre Sarah Bernhardt, Paris, June 6, 1928.

The creation of *Ode* belongs to a period
when Diaghilev was beginning to take a passionate interest in early Russian history and
to build a library of old Russian books.

He met Nabokov in Paris in the spring of 1927, and was immediately enthusiastic
about his intention of composing a score to an ode by the eighteenth-century Russian poet
Lomonosov, eulogist of the Empress Elizabeth Petrovna.

Having decided to present *Ode* in dance form, Diaghilev asked me to adapt a scenario to
Nabokov's music, and for the mise-en-scène he approached Tchelitchev.

Diaghilev and I had met Tchelitchev in Berlin, in 1923, and it was at my instigation
that Tchelitchev had that same year come to take up residence in Paris. In Germany he
had executed several stage designs for ballet and theatre productions, but he had since given
up the theatre to devote himself to painting; as he put it, he wanted to "learn how to paint
again." This was the first time in five years that he had collaborated on a work for the
theatre.

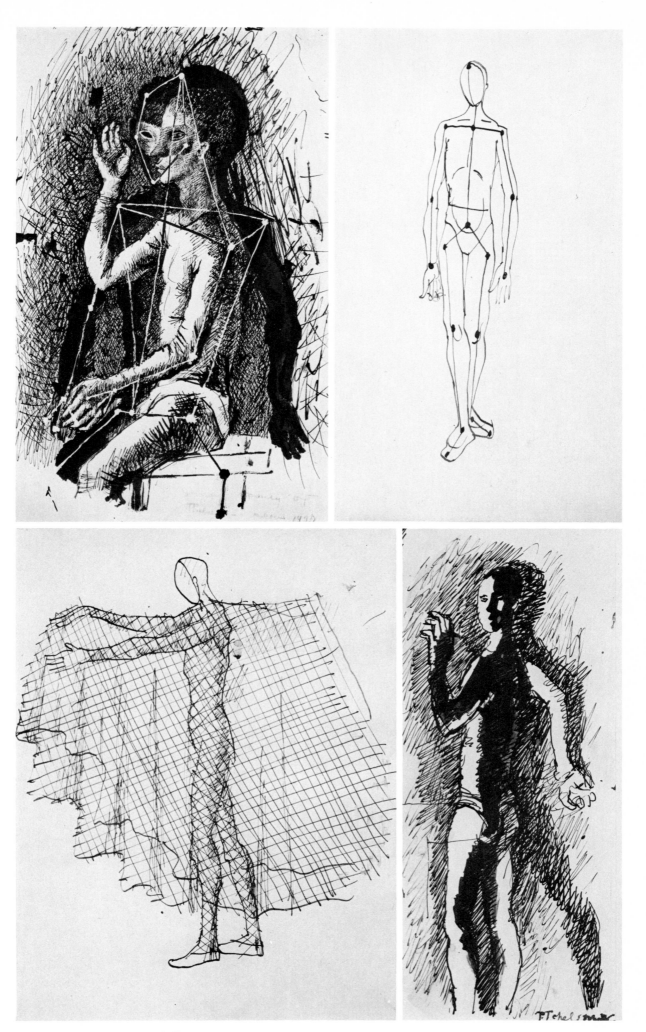

Sketches for *Ode*, by Pavel Tchelitchev

Irina Beliankina,
by Picasso

———

Woizikowski,
Domansky, and
Borovsky in *Ode*

Diaghilev wanted the scenic elements of *Ode* to be based on eighteenth-century allegorical drawings—on engravings of Court balls and the coronation festivities of the Empress Elizabeth. While agreeing to go along with this concept and to make use of documents of the period, Tchelitchev also wanted to express himself in a language that was his own, and to use modern technical devices in his mise-en-scène. He introduced into his plans for *Ode* elements that were incompatible with a strict historical reconstruction—cinematic projections, neon lighting, and phosphorescent costumes.

When Diaghilev saw that Tchelitchev was moving away from the initial concept of the production, he lost interest and asked me to take over the supervision of the assorted work in progress for *Ode*.

Tchelitchev was extremely high-strung and quite incompetent in the matter of film techniques, so that the atmosphere of our collaboration was dramatic. The indescribable chaos of the dress rehearsal—the first and only rehearsal in which the various elements that normally comprise a performance were brought together—justified my fear of a disastrous première.

The complexity of Tchelitchev's set, the impossibility of lighting the dancers during the film-projection sequence, the dismay of the company on learning that the ballet score was being sung, the troubles of Irina Beliankina, Stravinsky's niece, who was making her debut in the leading (mimed) role—all these hampered the progress of the dress rehearsal and caused violent arguments.

The rehearsal had begun the evening of June 5; it ended at noon the next day, which enabled us to correct the sets and the lighting. We worked right up until the moment when the theatre doors were opened to the audience. And it was then we learned that the Prefecture of Police forbade the use of neon lights as fire hazards.

Throughout those hours of anguish, only Diaghilev remained imperturbable; he never interfered in our discussions, as if he wanted to test my abilities as leader of the team.

Contrary to my fears, the première of *Ode* went off without the slightest mishap, and Diaghilev's approving smile at the end of the performance convinced me of the success of our perilous undertaking.

LE
PAS D'ACIER

Ballet in two scenes by Serge Prokofiev, Georges Yakoulov, and Leonide Massine. Music by Prokofiev. Choreography by Massine. Constructions and costumes after designs by Yakoulov. First performance: Théâtre Sarah Bernhardt, Paris, June 7, 1927.

After his last visit to Moscow and St. Petersburg in 1914, Diaghilev had lost all direct touch with Russia, but he was passionately interested in news of his country's artistic life and in Soviet theatre productions. In 1922, when he met Vladimir Mayakovsky in Berlin, the Russian poet had just arrived from Moscow. Diaghilev questioned him endlessly about the development of Russian art since the Revolution and about the young revolutionary theatre. He did the same when they met later in Paris. (Diaghilev had intervened to help Mayakovsky obtain a visa to visit France.)

On his arrival, Mayakovsky had talked euphorically of the new Russia's cultural progress and its artistic achievements, but then he discovered contemporary Western art. Back in Moscow, he wrote me a letter signed "Your poor provincial, Mayakovsky."

The Paris season of Taïrov's Kamerny Theatre, which came from Moscow in 1923, gave Diaghilev his first glimpse of theatrical trends in the U.S.S.R. and of the Constructivist stage sets of Exter and Yakoulov. He was most enthusiastic about these productions, decided

Конструкция декорации состоит из 4х частей. 1) неподвижная площадка для балетной работы, 2) бутафорская (станок с педалью) мелкая единица на колёсах – подвижная, 3) спускающиеся сверху на валах колёса 4) спускающиеся сверху бутафорско-осветительные приборы. В целях экономии передвигающиеся приборы (снаряды) будут рассчитаны на обслуживание ряда действий. Количество будет сведено к минимуму.

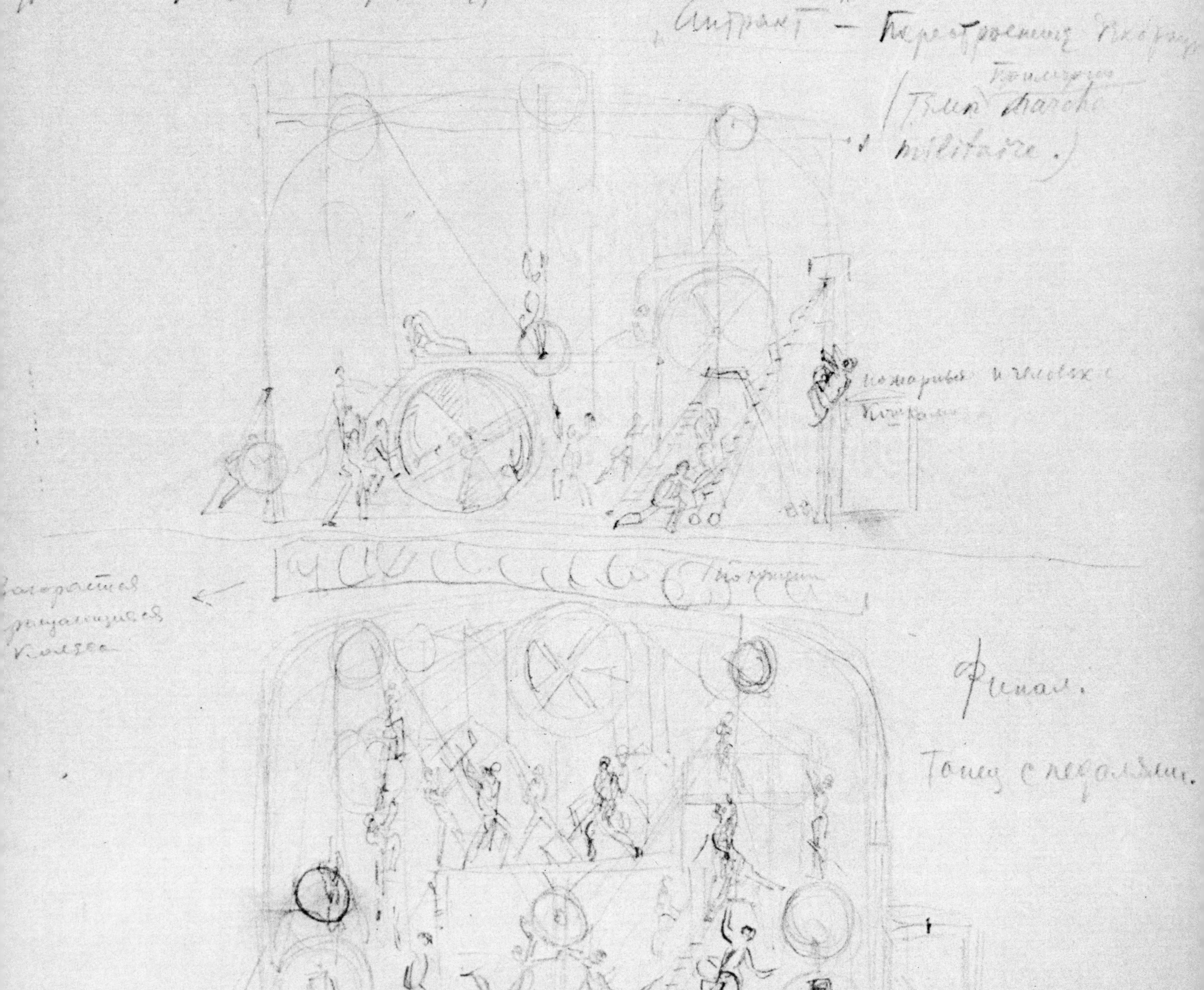

"Антракт" – Перестроение экзерг[.]
(Вид траки Теплушка
military.)

пожарные и членов
Бригады

загорается
двигающееся
колесо

→ Люди

Финал.
Танец с педалями.

that he would create a "Soviet ballet," and commissioned Prokofiev to write the score.

Diaghilev hoped to entrust the staging of his new ballet to a Soviet artist and choreographer, and also to complete the usual staff of collaborators in a dance production by bringing a theatrical director from Russia.

In 1925, when Yakoulov was in Paris on a visit, Diaghilev asked him to design the sets and costumes for the new ballet, and to collaborate with Prokofiev on his scenario. Initially, Prokofiev called the ballet *Ursignol*—a title derived from the abbreviation "U.R.S.S." and parodying the title of Stravinsky's *Rossignol*—but Diaghilev disliked this derisive note and, in the end, the ballet was called *Le Pas d'Acier*.

Yakoulov recommended that Larionov be appointed stage manager for *Le Pas d'Acier*, but Diaghilev instructed him to enter into negotiations with Taïrov and Meyerhold. On his return to Moscow in the autumn of 1925, Yakoulov got in touch with Taïrov, who declined Diaghilev's offer, claiming urgent commitments in the U.S.S.R. As for Meyerhold, he answered Yakoulov with a laconic letter in which he said that "for several reasons" he could not accept Diaghilev's proposal. Diaghilev's efforts to secure the collaboration of Kasian Goleizovsky or other young Soviet choreographers also came to nothing.

When all these attempts failed, Yakoulov's help notwithstanding, Diaghilev realized he would have to give up his hope of obtaining Soviet talent and approach his old collaborators. He abandoned the idea of having a special director and turned over to Massine the entire work of choreographer and director for the new ballet.

Parisians awaited *Le Pas d'Acier* with considerable curiosity, anticipating a Bolshevik propaganda ballet. However, it gave rise to no protests at the première or at later per-

Model for set for *Le Pas d'Acier*

formances at the Sarah Bernhardt and was a unanimous success. The only incident this ballet provoked took place in the wings the evening of the première, and it was due to a misunderstanding.

Vladimir Dukelsky overheard Cocteau criticizing the choreography; mistaking the target of his attacks, Dukelsky interrupted with some impertinence and insulted Cocteau, who lost his habitual restraint and slapped him. This scene took place in semidarkness backstage, and for the moment passed unnoticed, but the next day I received the following letter from Cocteau:

My dear Boris:

I very much regret having caused a disturbance on Serge's stage, but, given Dima's mug, his rose, his top hat and his Louis XV cane, his denunciation of Parisian frivolity was hard to take.

I did give him a good smack. His only response was a rather odd "That's all right" and a shameful flight via the nearest exit. He shielded himself at the stage door by offering his arm to a "lady." He escaped under a hail of jibes and laughter from a small crowd of musicians and dancers.

Do tell Serge how much I regret this incident. It was inevitable. My affectionate greetings,

Jean

P.S. My views were of an aesthetic and also of a moral order. I do reproach Massine for having turned something as great as the Russian Revolution into a cotillion-like spectacle within the intellectual grasp of ladies who pay six thousand francs for a box. I was not attacking the composer or the stage designer.

Scenes from *Le Pas d'Acier*

On June 13, I received another letter from Cocteau, which put an end to this incident.

June 13, 1926
10 Rue d'Anjou

My dear Boris:

Dukelsky came to see me day before yesterday before the performance, and he swore to me that never had he uttered the words I heard him utter.

In view of this position, I withdrew the slap (to whatever extent one can withdraw a slap).

There are differences of class, differences in the skies in which this one lives or that one lives, watertight compartments. I grow more and more indulgent. That slap was a reflex, nothing more—the thousandth of a second in which the Angel Heartbreak hovers in the air.

The Soviet Embassy has invited me to a Garden-Party [sic]. The G.P. postponed a fortnight following the murder of Woïkoff. Dima's rose, his cane, and Le Pas d'Acier *have now received their official apologies. Poor Lenin!*

Affectionate greetings,

Jean

APOLLON MUSAGETE

Ballet in two scenes by Igor Stravinsky. Choreography by George Balanchine. Décor and costumes by André Bauchant. First performance by the Ballets Russes: Théâtre Sarah Bernhardt, Paris, June 12, 1928.

Before Diaghilev presented *Apollon Musagète* in Europe, in a version choreographed by Balanchine, the ballet was performed at the Library of Congress, in Washington, D.C., on April 27, 1928. It had been commissioned by a group of wealthy American patrons, the score was written by Stravinsky, and the initial choreography created by Adolph Bolm.

Apollon Musagète—a "play without a plot," as Stravinsky wrote in a note for the Ballets Russes program—was simply a series of dance solos. As such, it offered unlimited scope to Balanchine's choreographic inventiveness and permitted him to establish a personal plastic style that came to be termed "neoclassic." The ballet was based on the techniques of the academic school, and it was interpreted by the "classical" premiers danseurs of the company—Lifar, Nikitina (alternating with Danilova), Doubrovska, and Tchernicheva.

Diaghilev commissioned André Bauchant to design the mise-en-scène, dealing through the Jeanne Bucher Gallery, where he had first seen the artist's work.

We never did meet Bauchant; he lived in the country and never came to town. And although he had accepted Diaghilev's commission, he never delivered any sketches. Diaghilev then decided to use for the sets the landscapes from two of Bauchant's canvases, which Prince Schervashidze adapted for the stage.

As for costumes, Bauchant confessed he was incapable of designing them, so Diaghilev copied Apollo's tunic from the costume of a figure in one of Bauchant's mythological compositions, and he dressed the three Muses in muslin tutus; later these were replaced by costumes designed by Gabrielle Chanel.

THE GODS
GO A-BEGGING

Pastoral ballet by Sobeka. Music by Handel, arranged by Sir Thomas Beecham. Choreography by George Balanchine. Décor by Léon Bakst (from *Daphnis et Chloë*). Costumes by Juan Gris (from *Les Tentations de la Bergère*). First performance: His Majesty's Theatre, London, July 16, 1928. Principal dancers: Alexandra Danilova, Lubov Tchernicheva, Felia Doubrovska, Léon Woizikowski, Constantin Tcherkas.

In 1928, on the eve of the Ballets Russes performances in London, Diaghilev, discovering that there were not enough ballets for the season about to begin, decided to produce straightaway a new ballet based on a suite of symphonic pieces by Handel, put together by Sir Thomas Beecham. I had adapted for Handel's music a theme inspired by eighteenth-century pastoral allegories, and Balanchine had worked out the choreography in a few days.

Because lack of time made it impossible to have a new mise-en-scène prepared, Diaghilev used for *The Gods Go A-begging* the costumes Juan Gris had designed for *Les Tentations de la Bergère* and Bakst's décor for the first and third scenes of *Daphnis et Chloë*. Despite the speed with which the ballet had been conceived and completed, *The Gods Go A-begging* was a great triumph, its success due in great part to the brilliant interpretations of Danilova and Woizikowski.

Pierrot

Costume design by Juan Gris

LE BAL

Ballet in two scenes by Boris Kochno. Music by Vittorio Rieti. Choreography by George Balanchine. Décor and costumes by Giorgio de Chirico. First performance: Casino, Monte Carlo, May 9, 1929.

The scenario I wrote for *Le Bal* was based on a Hoffmannesque short story by Count Vladimir Sologub, a Russian author of the Romantic era. Accordingly, Diaghilev's initial intention was to place the action of the ballet in Russia, in the early 1800's. He found no artist capable of carrying out this idea, and so he approached de Chirico. Without recreating a definite period style, de Chirico devised a mise-en-scène that suggested a strange masked ball and accentuated the phantom-like aspect of the ballet's characters.

While Rieti was composing the music for *Le Bal*, Diaghilev intervened constantly and made him rewrite the music for several dances. When he sent on the score in its final form, Rieti accompanied it with a letter dated February 27, 1929:

Dear Monsieur Diaghilev:

Here is Le Bal. *It is dedicated to you. It is yours. Do with it what you like, but never suppose that I am going to work on it further.*

Yours, as always,
*Vittorio Rieti**

Anton Dolin had returned to the company in 1929, and Diaghilev, wishing to give him a place in the troupe equivalent to Lifar's, entrusted him with the leading role in *Le Bal*. His partner was Danilova.

One of the early performances of *Le Bal* in Monte Carlo was upset by Danilova's sudden lapse of memory. As she was about to begin her variation, she forgot the steps she was to dance, and, unable to improvise, she ran offstage.

---

* This letter appears in *The Diaghilev Ballet: 1909–1929*, by Serge Grigoriev, London, Constable, 1953.

Scenes from *Le Bal*

THE
PRODIGAL SON

Ballet in three scenes by Boris Kochno. Music by Serge Prokofiev. Choreography by George Balanchine. Décor and costumes by Georges Rouault. First performance: Théâtre Sarah Bernhardt, Paris, May 21, 1929.

In 1927, immediately after the production of *La Pas d'Acier*, Diaghilev asked Prokofiev to write a new ballet for the company. He had no specific theme to suggest, and his great preoccupation at the time was to find one. He wanted the new work to be simple and easy to follow, unlike Prokofiev's earlier ballets, and not to require a cumbersome set. He was looking for a timeless theme, a poetic episode that would be universally familiar and could serve as the unifying thread for a suite of dances, and yet impose no definite period or place on the artists creating the ballet.

To find a subject that satisfied all these conditions was not easy. Time passed. Prokofiev grew impatient while waiting for the scenario Diaghilev was to submit to him. He was on the point of giving up the commission when I had the idea of a theatrical version of the parable of the prodigal son.

Later, in the first published edition of the score for *Le Fils Prodigue*, Prokofiev omitted my name, and in order to have my paternity acknowledged I had to go to law. The verdict was in my favor, and the court ordered the first edition destroyed.

When the score for *Le Fils Prodigue* was finished, Diaghilev commissioned the mise-en-scène from Henri Matisse. He delegated the responsibility for introducing Prokofiev's music to Matisse to his orchestral conductor, Henri Defosse, and wired Matisse from England on August 31, 1928:

HENRY [*sic*] MATISSE, 92, ROUTE CLAMART, ISSY-LES-MOULINEAUX, PARIS. DEFOSSE INFORMS ME OF YOUR GOOD IMPRESSION OF MUSIC. DELIGHTED IF YOU WILLING DESIGN THE TWO BALLETS BEGINNING WITH SCHÉHÉRAZADE WHICH INTEND TO RESTAGE THIS WINTER. LETTER FOLLOWS. WARMEST GREETINGS. DIAGHILEV.

Diaghilev had decided to revamp the mise-en-scène and the mimed role of Schéhérazade after seeing a matinee performance by the company at the Casino that spring. He had mingled with the audience and followed the performance from the back of the hall, perched on a folding chair. Came the high point, the death scene of Zobeide. Diaghilev found it so outmoded and absurdly melodramatic that he was seized by paroxysms of laughter and his seat collapsed under him. Still on the floor, he went on laughing, to the indignation of the audience around him.

Yet the mere title *Schéhérazade*—one of the first triumphs of the Ballets Russes—was magic. During the company's tours abroad, it assured sold-out houses in advance, and every theatre manager who engaged the Diaghilev company asked for this ballet. So, since it was impossible to withdraw it from the repertoire, Diaghilev resolved to rejuvenate it: he would have Balanchine revise Fokine's dated and burlesque pantomime, and he would replace Bakst's now dingy set and worn costumes with a new mise-en-scène by Matisse.

As for *Le Fils Prodigue*, Matisse seemed to him the ideal painter for the setting of the ballet. Diaghilev hoped to secure his collaboration without difficulty, for Matisse had attended a rehearsal of *Chout* in 1921, had been interested in Prokofiev's music, and, in Nice that same year, had done a portrait of Prokofiev on Diaghilev's commission. Unfortunately, the original of this portrait, which was reproduced in the Ballets Russes program and also appeared (reprinted from the program) in my book, *Le Ballet*, was left behind in Diaghilev's room when we left the Hôtel Continental in 1921, and it was never found.

Matisse declined the new commission, however, despite the intervention of Prokofiev and other mutual friends; he said that working for the theatre was too absorbing and taxing, and would prevent his concentrating on his own painting.

After this refusal, on my advice Diaghilev asked Georges Rouault to do the mise-en-

scène for *Le Fils Prodigue*. Rouault agreed immediately and, on Diaghilev's invitation, promised to come to Monte Carlo, bringing his sketches with him. He arrived without the promised designs, but, he said, he had brought the necessary materials to execute them quickly on the spot.

He was staying at one of the hotels where Diaghilev lodged his guests—I do not remember whether it was the Hôtel de Paris or the Hermitage—and every morning he would come to the rehearsal studio and spend hours watching the dancing lessons and rehearsals. Every day he lunched with us at the Café de Paris, and after lunch closeted himself until evening in his room, where supposedly he was working.

Our lunches were a great bore, for Rouault was obsessed by the enthusiasm of his dealer, Ambroise Vollard, for the work of Marc Chagall, whom Rouault considered his rival. He talked of nothing but this "betrayal" and came to life only when he was sarcastically retelling the same stories over and over. He scarcely took part in any other conversation, and when *Le Fils Prodigue* was mentioned, he became mute.

Scenes from
The Prodigal Son

One day, after having watched Rouault drag on in Monte Carlo without giving the slightest evidence of any work, Diaghilev, at the end of his patience, resolved to get hold of the sketches which Rouault kept saying had been finished long since. He persuaded Rouault to take a drive along the Grande Corniche, rented a cab for him (asking the driver to prolong the usual excursion), and, in his absence, had his hotel room opened.

Diaghilev returned from this trespass empty-handed and wild-eyed. He had searched everywhere, turned the room upside down, and had discovered not one ballet sketch, indeed no trace whatever of any work. He had not even found sketching paper and had seen neither brushes nor colors.

That evening, Diaghilev announced to Rouault that a reservation had been made for him on the Paris train for the next day. He said nothing whatever about *Le Fils Prodigue*. Although Rouault had arrived with a single piece of luggage, he now seemed anxious to go up to his room to pack his bags, and he disappeared for the entire evening.

The following morning, before boarding the train, Rouault brought Diaghilev a stack of sketches for *Le Fils Prodigue*—admirable gouaches and pastels which he had executed in one night.

———————

The last season of the Ballets Russes in Paris, in 1929, attracted a new public—unfashionable but young and enthusiastic. During previous seasons, everyone in the boxes and orchestra knew each other, and people chatted among themselves as if they were in a private drawing room. This year, the theatre was invaded by a nameless crowd for whom the dance seemed to be a discovery, and they applauded the performers warmly.

One evening, a guest of Diaghilev's who had long been an habituée of Ballets Russes performances, entered her box at the end of an intermission and looked out over the theatre packed with unfamiliar faces. "Why, there's no one here!" she said, in great disappointment, and left immediately for a première in another theatre where she hoped to find "people."

AUGUST 19, 1929

T he illness of which Diaghilev was to die, diabetes, was disclosed by his friend and physician, Dr. Dalimier, in the spring of 1929.

Dalimier had attended Diaghilev regularly for several years; haunted by fears of purely imaginary illnesses, Diaghilev used to go see him or telephone him at all hours of the day and night.

In token of his gratitude for the doctor's friendly devotion, in 1926 Diaghilev had presented him with a portrait of Dalimier's children, which he had commissioned from Pedro Pruna. When ordering the portrait, Diaghilev had suggested that Pruna draw on the style of the Renaissance painters, but Pruna had retorted, "Mantegna will remain Mantegna, and there will be no fake Mantegnas signed Pruna!"

(I have seen Pruna "correct" the works of Old Masters; working from photographs, he would alter the positions of the figures.)

When Diaghilev heard the doctor's diagnosis, he was alarmed, and as long as he was in Paris— in May and June of 1929—he consulted Dalimier almost daily; he made him listen at length to his heart and lungs, and asked many questions about his illness. But—unlike his behavior in the case of a mild, not to say nonexistent, illness—when Diaghilev left Dalimier's office, he seemed to forget his instructions, and followed only those that interfered least with his habits.

After he arrived in London in June for the Ballets Russes season, Diaghilev felt sicker and sicker, took to his bed, and very rarely came to the performances at Covent Garden, where he had put me in charge.

Back in Paris at the end of July, Diaghilev resumed his visits to Dalimier, who was visibly anxious about his patient's condition and prescribed a stay of several weeks in a clinic or rest home.

Diaghilev disregarded the doctor's warnings, and early in August he left with Igor Markevich for a vacation in Austria and Germany.

Later, I learned that during this trip Diaghilev, determined not to admit he was ill or restrict himself in any way, had led a life he hadn't the strength for, which had hastened his death.

In Salzburg, Munich, and Baden-Baden, he would rise early, go off on tourist excursions and,

in the afternoons, attend festival rehearsals. He would return to his hotel room in the early evening, only to change and go out again to the theatre or to a concert.

Back at his hotel by midnight, Diaghilev, exhausted, would fall asleep for a few minutes, then get up, put on his dinner jacket again, and go down to the restaurant; waking up the hotel help, he would order a supper consisting of dishes that were strictly forbidden.

After ten days of this "return to youth," Diaghilev took leave of Markevich and went on to Venice, where he was to meet Lifar.

I was on vacation in Toulon, and there I received three wires from Diaghilev, all within twenty-four hours. The first, dated August 14, read: THE WEATHER IS BEAUTIFUL DO NOT FORGET ME.

The next morning, Diaghilev telegraphed me: HEALTH NOT VERY GOOD WHEN DO YOU PLAN ON COMING?

And the evening of that same day: AM SICK COME AT ONCE DIAGHILEV.

I left Toulon immediately and arrived the evening of the sixteenth at the Hôtel des Bains, on the Lido, where Diaghilev and Lifar were staying.

The doctor recommended by the hotel management was in Diaghilev's room when I entered.

Diaghilev was in bed, very pale and nervous. He was deep in conversation with the doctor and scarcely noticed my presence. Later, he talked to me in anguish about the wretched state of his health and the incompetence of this Venetian physician, who hesitated to confirm Dalimier's diagnosis, wandered off into the vaguest speculations, and came to see him only to find out how much worse his illness was.

However, the next morning when I came into Diaghilev's sunny bedroom, I found him relaxed and smiling, which might have led one to believe in a sudden turn for the better. When we were alone, Diaghilev spoke to me rapturously about his recent trip.

He seemed enchanted to have escaped for ten days from a life that was becoming burdensome to him, an existence dominated by work and filled with obligations. He seemed to have made a marvelous return to the past, to the years of his youth. As he talked to me about his "rediscovery of Wag-

Diaghilev's tomb in Venice

ner's genius," he gave me the impression that he was moving away from ballet.

Diaghilev's relaxed mood reassured me. I went off until evening and, on coming back to the hotel, learned that Misia Sert and Chanel had visited him. Diaghilev was very animated, and, as he spoke of them, he kept saying, "They were so young, all in white! They were so white!"

During the evening, Diaghilev's temperature went up, and I decided to spend the night in his room. Until the morning, he was very disturbed. One moment he was shivering; the next moment he complained that he was suffocating from the heat. He felt as if he were in a draft, and every other minute he would ask me to open or close the window and door. At dawn, before dropping off to sleep, he murmured, "Forgive me. . . ."

When he awoke, Diaghilev was calm, but he felt tired and talked of nothing except rest and vacation in Naples and Sicily.

Toward evening, he seemed to be dozing. Trusting to the watchful attention of the nurse, I went to my room and, worn out from my vigil of the night before, fell asleep instantly. Around midnight, I was awakened by Lifar, who urged me to go back to Diaghilev.

I found Diaghilev stretched out on his back, his eyes closed; he was breathing loud and hard, as if his chest were lifting a tremendous weight. The nurse was packing her bag. When she was ready to leave, she said calmly, "Sick people in that condition last till dawn."

I had the doctor awakened; when he arrived, he could only say that Diaghilev's condition was desperate.

Misia Sert, hurrying over from Venice in response to my telephone call, summoned a priest. We asked him to recite the prayer very quickly, for we were afraid that Diaghilev would regain consciousness and would be upset by the presence of a priest.

After a death agony that lasted several hours, Diaghilev stopped breathing. The first rays of the sun came through the window and touched his forehead. His head sank toward his shoulder, and a tear rolled down his cheek.

It was six o'clock in the morning of August 19, 1929.

AUTOBIOGRAPHICAL
NOTES BY
SERGE
DIAGHILEV

These autobiographical notes,
which Diaghilev dictated to me in 1922 and
which are transcribed verbatim, indicate to which stages
of his artistic activity he attached the
greatest importance. BORIS KOCHNO

Serge de Diaghilev was born March 19, 1872, on a country estate near Novgorod. His father, a regimental officer of the Horse Guards, was on friendly terms with Moussorgsky, Tchaikovsky, and Leskov.

Diaghilev attended the gymnasium in Perm, in the Urals, where his parents owned land and factories.

Arriving in St. Petersburg in 1890, Diaghilev completed his law studies at the University in 1896 and, in 1898, his courses at the Conservatory, where he studied singing with Professor Cotogni and musical theory (composition) with N. Sokolov and A. Liadov.

In 1897, Diaghilev began to contribute art criticism to the daily newspaper *Les Nouvelles*. That same year, he organized an exhibition of English and German water-colorists.

In 1898, Diaghilev was appointed by Prince d'Oldenburg to organize in St. Petersburg an exhibition of Scandinavian painters.

In 1899, Diaghilev founded and directed the magazine *World of Art (Mir Isskoustva)*, which was published for six years. The first year, the magazine's patrons were Princess Tenichev and S. I. Mamontov; for the next five years, the funds for the publication were supplied by Czar Nicholas II. The same year the magazine was founded, Diaghilev began organizing annual *World of Art*

Photograph of
Pavlova and Fokine in the
Yearbook of the
Imperial Theatres

Chaliapin,
by Serov, 1905

exhibitions; in all, sixteen shows were presented in St. Petersburg, Moscow, Berlin, Cologne, Düsseldorf, Darmstadt, and Venice.

In 1900–1, Diaghilev was editor in chief of the *Annual Report of the Imperial Theatres.*

In 1904, Diaghilev published a study of the painter Dmitri G. Levitzky, which won the Uvarov Grand Prize, awarded by the Academy of Sciences. Simultaneously, he brought out a collection (monograph) of the works of Levitan and an album of lithographs by Russian artists.

In 1905, Diaghilev was appointed to organize a historical exhibition of Russian portraits, including almost twenty-five hundred works, which was held at the Tavrida Palace. The exhibition was under the patronage of the Czar. The president of the organizing committee was the Grand Duke Nicholas Mikhailovich.

In 1906, Diaghilev began his artistic activities abroad. In October, he organized an exhibition of Russian painters in Paris, which was shown at the Fall Salon in the Grand Palais. This was followed, in 1907, by the "*Concerts Historiques Russes,*" with the personal participation of Rimsky-Korsakov, Glazounov, Scriabin, Rachmaninov, Nikisch, and others. It was at these concerts that Chaliapin made his Paris debut.

In 1908, Diaghilev produced Moussorgsky's *Boris Godunov* at the Paris Opéra, for the first time outside Russia, with Chaliapin, Smirnov, and other Russian singers, as well as Blumenfeldt (orchestra conductor) and the choruses of the Imperial Theatre of Moscow.

In 1909, at the Théâtre du Châtelet, in Paris, Diaghilev staged *The Maid of Pskov*, by Rimsky-Korsakov, with Chaliapin, Lipkovska, and the orchestra and chorus of the Moscow Opera; and he presented the first season of the Ballets Russes, with Nijinsky, Pavlova, Karsavina, Fokine, and Mordkin. The program included the first act of Glinka's *Russlan and Ludmila*, the third act of Borodin's *Prince Igor*, *Les Sylphides*, *Cléopâtre*, etc. That same year, Diaghilev commissioned *Daphnis et Chloë* from Ravel and *The Firebird* from Stravinsky.

In 1910, Ballets Russes season at the Paris Opéra. First Berlin season. *Firebird*, *Schéhérazade*, *Carnaval*. Diaghilev commissions *Petrouchka* from Stravinsky. In 1911, Ballets Russes season at the International Exposition of Rome and third season in Paris (Châtelet). *Petrouchka*, *Spectre de la Rose*. First London season, at Covent Garden, which opens during the coronation ceremonies of King George V.

Diaghilev commissions *Le Sacre du Printemps* from Stravinsky.

In 1912—the Ballets Russes in Paris, at the Théâtre du Châtelet. *Daphnis et Chloë*, *L'Après-Midi d'un Faune*. Diaghilev commissions *Jeux* from Debussy.

In 1913—a Russian season of opera and ballet at the Théâtre des Champs-Élysées. *Le Sacre du Printemps*, *Jeux*, and other ballets. *Khovanshchina*, *Boris Godunov* (Chaliapin, choruses of the Maryinsky Theatre). In the autumn, the Ballets Russes makes their debut in Latin America. Diaghilev commissions *The Legend of Joseph* from Richard Strauss.

In 1914—a season of opera and ballet at the Paris Opéra. *Le Rossignol, Coq d'Or, Joseph* (with Strauss conducting).

Concurrently, in the years 1912–14, Diaghilev produces, at London's Covent Garden and Drury Lane Theatre, seasons of Russian operas and ballets that include, in addition to *Boris Godunov* (Chaliapin's first appearance in London), *Khovanshchina, The Maid of Pskov, Coq d'Or, Le Rossignol, Prince Igor,* and *May Night.*

In 1915—a benefit gala at the Paris Opéra, with *The Midnight Sun.* This same year, Diaghilev brings Prokofiev to Rome, and commissions him to compose *Chout (Le Bouffon).*

In 1916—the first tour of the Ballets Russes in North America, engagement at the Metropolitan Opera in New York. First season of the Ballets Russes in Madrid (by command of His Majesty, Alfonso XIII). Second United States tour.

This same year, Diaghilev commissions a ballet *(Parade)* from Satie and Picasso, and another *(The Three-Cornered Hat)* from de Falla, and organizes a concert at the Augusteo, in Rome.

In 1917—a season at the Rome Opera and at the Châtelet, in Paris. *The Good-Humored Ladies, Parade.* Second tour in Latin America and final appearance of Nijinsky with the Ballets Russes (September 26, 1917). Diaghilev commissions *Le Chant du Rossignol* from Stravinsky.

In 1918—the opening of a season in London that, with short interruptions, lasts from August, 1918, until December, 1919: fifty-five weeks.

1917–18—After extensive research in the archives of Naples, Rome, and Milan and studying the work of Cimarosa, Paisiello, and Pergolesi, Diaghilev assembles some musical fragments by the latter into a ballet, *Pulcinella,* for the arrangement of which he commissions Stravinsky.

Diaghilev,
by Bakst, 1905

—————

Exhibition of
Russian art, Paris, 1906,
"Salon d'Automne"; gallery
decorated by Bakst

1920—Ballets Russes season in London (Covent Garden) and three seasons in Paris: the first, January–February; the second, May–July, at the Opéra *(Chant du Rossignol,* H. Matisse; *Pulcinella, The Three-Cornered Hat,* Picasso; *Boutique Fantasque,* A. Derain); and, in December, a season at the Théâtre des Champs-Élysées.

1921—Season in Paris, at the Gaîté-Lyrique *(Le Bouffon, Cuadro Flamenco,* Picasso). Season in London, June–July. He commissions the opera *Mavra* from Stravinsky.

End 1921—*The Sleeping Beauty,* in London. Uncut version for first time abroad. A hundred and fifteen consecutive performances. First appearance of Spessivtzeva in London.

1922—Ballets Russes season at the Paris Opéra *(Mavra, Renard).* Same year, he commissions Poulenc for *Les Biches,* Auric for *Les Fâcheux,* and Satie and Prokofiev for new ballets.

—————————

Diaghilev's notes stop here.

I am supplementing them with a word about several of his projects that never reached production, but about which he talked to me and jotted down some indications in his notebooks.

In 1922, together with Jean Cocteau, Diaghilev was working on plans for a series of Plastic-Hall performances—avant-garde music-hall dance performances—to be produced with members of the Ballets Russes. The programs of this international youth theatre were to consist chiefly of dance numbers, ballet excerpts, and screenings of experimental films.

In 1923, Diaghilev attempted without success to found an arts center in the Principality of Monaco. His plans called for creating a Museum of Modern Art in Monaco (portraits of the Royal Family to be commissioned from Picasso); the Palais des Beaux Arts de Monte-Carlo (then being used as a variety theatre) to be remodeled, after plans by Braque, into exhibition halls; annual festivals of international music, opera, ballet, etc.

These plans were submitted to the directors of the Société des Bains de Mer, but, despite the intervention of the Prince of Monaco, they were never approved.

In 1929, shortly before his death, Diaghilev commissioned two new ballets for what was to have been the next season of the Ballets Russes, in 1930; they were based on scenarios by Boris Kochno. Paul Hindemith was commissioned to write the score for *No. 27*, and Igor Markevich the score for *L'Habit du Roi*.

Notes for the "Plastic Hall" productions of avant-garde choreography, from Diaghilev's notebook, 1922

Diaghilev's reply to the London press:

Sir:

Having read the London press on my most recent production, Chout, *by MM. Prokofiev and Larionov, and in particular such papers as the* Sunday Times, Westminster Gazette, Daily Express, *and* Daily News, *I permit myself some melancholy reflections on the value of the following opinions.*

Nothing is more dangerous, really, than to express an opinion.

How frightened I used to be by every critical opinion of my actions. How frightened I am now that no opinion terrifies me any more!

One cause for panic persists—the existence of that pitiless law decreeing that everyone everywhere should misunderstand for the same reason and in the same way.

Mankind can invent airplanes and telephones, but with the help of those telephones men will keep on telling each other the same stupid things about every new idea and new development.

When I was sixteen, I heard someone say that not a single melody was to be found in all of Wagner; at twenty, I was told that Rimsky-Korsakov's music was mere mathematics; at twenty-five, that Cézanne and Gauguin were frauds. As for Debussy! Strauss! Le Douanier Rousseau! Matisse! For fifteen years people hooted at them, without even suspecting they were making fools of themselves.

In my own art of the dance, Fokine battled with the elderly Petipa and was choreography's revolutionary flag-bearer, yet he was so revolted by the "ugliness" of Nijinsky's Après-Midi d'un Faune *that after the première he insisted on having his name removed from the Ballets Russes poster.*

Diaghilev's French passport

In 1916, Mr. Otto Kahn, director of the Metropolitan Opera of New York, refused to accept Massine as premier danseur because "he didn't know how to dance"; and in 1911, Mr. Higgins, director of Covent Garden, begged me by letter to bring some ballerina other than Karsavina, who had "made too poor a showing in London."

It will be readily understood how stupid and banal it seems to me that the present learned critics are in their turn attacking Stravinsky and Picasso, Prokofiev and Larionov. Not even the example of Le Sacre du Printemps, *which in the space of seven years has passed from being hissed at to being* the event of modern music—*not even this has opened the eyes of these benighted people.*

My good friend Newman launches forth again with his monstrosities, saying that Stravinsky reminds him of Eric Fogg and reiterating that Prokofiev (whose sonorities are mere "street noise") is a musical "enfant terrible." In all candor, one can say that it is Newman, rather, who is the vieillard terrible *of criticism. This is all the more obvious today, when he would like to appear as a youthful avant-gardist himself. In the article "The Genius of Stravinsky," he finds* Petrouchka *"flat, formalistic and* démodé," *and with vast insouciance says the same of* Sacre du Printemps *(naughty old man!). We recognize the game, and also realize that, for his money, the man of the hour is Brahms—nor is he ashamed to admit it!*

Diaghilev's
Russian passport

In my fairly wide travels, I have never read such "démodé" articles with such "provincial" ideas as those of Newman. What a pity for such an amiable man. This year, he has a few white hairs. Why make those white hairs blush at the laughter of young people all over the world? Poor old friend, act with the dignity of your advancing years and do not align yourself with the fools who boo the première of Carmen *or the paintings of Manet or the poetry of Mallarmé.*

It is quite obvious that exactly the same thing is happening with Chout *as happened with* Petrouchka. *People protested bitterly against that earlier Stravinsky masterpiece, and even those best disposed considered it "caviar" for the gourmet members of the public.* Chout *will travel the road of all beautiful works of art. Its controversial reception proves as much.*

One critic very prudently said that he had made up his mind after hearing the Chout *score twice, at the dress rehearsal and at the première. I had wanted to thank the London press for its friendliness by arranging a special rehearsal in its honor. Now I fear the same thing has happened to several critics that once befell an elderly lady of my acquaintance. To make Scriabin's* Prometheus *easier to understand, the organizers of the concert had the work played twice in one evening. At the end of the first performance, my friend was enchanted with the music; after the second, she was in despair because she no longer understood it at all.*

This is the very thing—the total incomprehension of all these embarrassed critics—which causes me to see through their banal reactions, which I have listened to for twenty-five years, to every unfamiliar work. Poor, pious frauds, they are caught between orthodoxy and life—and in that predicament it is hard to avoid being ridiculous. But ridiculous is what they are and what they will always be.

June, 1921

Serge Diaghilev

DIAGHILEV
DISCUSSES
CLASSICAL DANCE

Unpublished text
of Diaghilev's interview with a reporter
from *La Renaissance*, a Russian-language paper
published in Paris. The interview took
place in December, 1928.

The art of the dance has moved away from classical canons, but it has not yet found a clear and defined style. At the moment, the dance is passing through a period of experimentation that, in recent years, has aroused lively controversy.

Which path would allow the dance to attain new heights? To wish the dance to return to pure classicism betrays a disregard of the present, say the innovators. The reply is: the dance does not exist outside its classic form. You are turning your back on the very art you serve.

This is the problem about which Diaghilev gives us his point of view:

Our concept of theatrical dance is of relatively recent origin.

Whereas painting and sculpture find their classical basis in a centuries-long experience, the classical school of ballet originated in the eighteenth century, and sprang into vigorous life in the course of the nineteenth. In the last century, the muslin tutu was standard for women, and it is this classical school which, unarguably, sets the rules for the choreography of our day.

If theatrical creativity is to evolve, however, it is not enough to remain faithful to our teachers. We were not taught algebra and ancient Greek in order to spend our lives solving problems or speaking the language of Sophocles.

Today, dance and choreography must, of course, get their graduation certificate from the classical school, but only in the sense in which a Picasso must have precise knowledge of human anatomy, or a Stravinsky would be forbidden to write parallel fifths while he was still a student.

Duncan, Dalcroze, Laban, and Wigman provide solid foundations for the quest for a new style. Their effort to heighten the possibilities of that sublime instrument which is the human body altogether deserves our approval. Yet their crusade against the "outdated" classical dance led choreography into a blind alley from which it has not yet escaped.

Germany has dancers who can move admirably, but they do not know how to dance.

None of this should lead us to conclude, however, that the road toward a modern choreography can be mapped by a misty-eyed attachment to classical forms.

Let me take an example from another field. People who defend such a point of view should join the society for the protection of ancient monuments but ought to abstain entirely from giving advice to contemporary architects.

A case in point: the gifted innovators who have created American skyscrapers would find it easy to restore arms to the Venus de Milo, because they have a profound knowledge of classical art.

But what, precisely, offends our eye in New York is the Greek portico of the Carnegie Library and the Doric columns of the railway stations.

Skyscrapers represent our classical art. Their lines, dimensions, and proportions are the expression of our classical endeavors. They are the true palaces of our period.

The situation with regard to choreography is of the same order. Our plastic and dynamic inventions must have a classical basis also, which allows every opportunity to search for new forms. These forms must be coherent and harmonious in their development, but far removed from a narrow, doctrinaire preachment of classicism.

In the work of today's choreographer, classicism must be the means, not the end.

And what do you think of Ida Rubinstein's attempts at classical dance?

Rubinstein's performance confirms what I have just been saying. It reveals the desire to cling to the traditions of classical ballet, but no coherence, no harmony, is ever apparent in her work.

Except for the ballet *David*, which Massine produced and in which one could discern a kind of choreographic structure, all her works are mere chaos, destitute of any creative imagination or the slightest new idea.

Rubinstein herself has not realized that classical dance is the most difficult, the most delicate, and the most ungrateful of all the arts. It does not forgive errors.

Her arched silhouette, her bent knees, the utter confusion in all her striving after a futile "classicism" largely account for the fact that a dancer in her company, of second rank but still knowing her job, looked to us like a star according to the old precepts of a routine invented half a century ago. When classical dance represents only a "monument of antiquity," one must not only *not* preserve it, one must condemn it, for it becomes a poison that can contaminate the organism of modern choreography.

That is how the "classicism" of Rubinstein's choreography looked to us, and I think I have the right to say so because, twenty years ago, it was I who introduced an exotic, mysterious, hieratic Ida Rubinstein to choreography.

How has she had the temerity to alter so mercilessly the image we had of her? To us that image seemed unforgettable, but she has erased it forever. Nothing is left but the debris, which does not even have the usual beauty of ruins silhouetted against the sky.

Boris Kochno, by Niki Ekstrom, Paris, 1968

INDEX

Page numbers in *italics* refer to pictures.
Text may be on the same pages.

Design by Bea Feitler
Contributor to Production: Carl Barile
Set in English Monotype Walbaum   Composed by Clarke & Way, Inc.
Printed by Connecticut Printers, Incorporated   Bound by American Book-Stratford Press, Inc.
Harper & Row, Publishers, Inc.

Le Pavillon d'Armide. Danses Polovtziennes du Prince Igor. Le Festin. Cléopâtre. Les Sylphides. Schéhérazade. Le Carnaval. Giselle. L'Oiseau de Feu. Les Orientales. Narcisse. Le Spectre de la Rose. Sadko. Petrouchka. Lac des Cygnes. Le Dieu Bleu. L'après-midi d'un Faune. Thamar. Daphnis et Chloë. Jeux. Le Sacre du Printemps. La Tragédie de Salomé. Papillons. La Légende de Joseph. Coq d'Or. Midas. Le Soleil de Nuit. Las Meninas.